basic Japanese cooking

jody vassallo

photographs by Clive Bozzard-Hill

basic

Japanese

cooking

whitecap

introduction

I have to say that Japanese cooking has taken the helm as my favourite Asian cuisine. It is fresh, healthy and relatively simple to prepare, and you don't need a thousand ingredients. Sushi does require a little practice and patience, but there are some fantastic step-by-step photographs at the beginning of this book that will guide you through preparing your own sushi. Remember practice is the key ingredient – sushi chefs train for a minimum of seven years in Japan. Making sushi is a great dinner party activity, so why not invite a few friends over and learn and laugh together. One of the best things about sushi is that even if you don't end up with a perfect looking roll, it will still taste amazing.

Another fantastic interactive dinner option is shabu shabu. Have a big pot of simmering water in the middle of the dinner table – an electric wok is perfect as it has a stable base and the heat can be easily controlled; fondue pots also work well – then give each guest a basket of vegetables and a plate of thinly sliced meat with pots of condiments and dipping sauces.

Soup is another healthy and satisfying meal. A large bowl of udon, ramen or soba noodles topped with vegetables and fish, chicken or meat only takes about ten minutes to prepare and tastes even better the next day as the noodles soak up some of the dashi-infused stock, so try and leave some for lunch.

For those who like simplicity and like to eat outdoors and cook on a barbecue, yakitori requires hardly any preparation – just soak a few bamboo skewers for 15 minutes or invest in a few metal ones, make the sauce and simply cook, turn and dip. Serve these with some of the wonderful salads that are included in the book and then finish the meal with one of the delicious sweet treats.

My proudest moment when testing the recipes for this book came when I emulated the chocolate black sesame cake I discovered at Tokyo railway station. You must make this recipe even if you don't try anything else in this book, as you will not be disappointed. Serve it with green tea ice cream and you will be in heaven.

This book contains a selection of recipes that will introduce you to the basics of Japanese cuisine. Share them with your friends and family or slurp a big bowl of noodles on your own. Enjoy.

ingredients

nori

sesame oil

rice vinegar

chili oil

brown rice

sushi rice

inari

bonito flakes

panko breadcrumbs

tempura flour

dried shrimp

tenkasu

dashi granules

kombu

sake

soy sauce

mirin

wakame

Japanese curry

ao nori

wasabi paste

shichimi togarashi powder

mustard powder

mayonnaise

wasabi powder

tonkatsu sauce

chili paste

eggplant   bamboo   pink ginger   salmon roe

pickled vegetables

daikon   spring onions   red ginger

umeboshi plums

flying fish roe

gyoza wrappers

seaweed salad

soft tofu

black sesame seeds

matcha

white sesame seeds

firm tofu

ginger root   pak choi   bok choy   Japanese eggplant

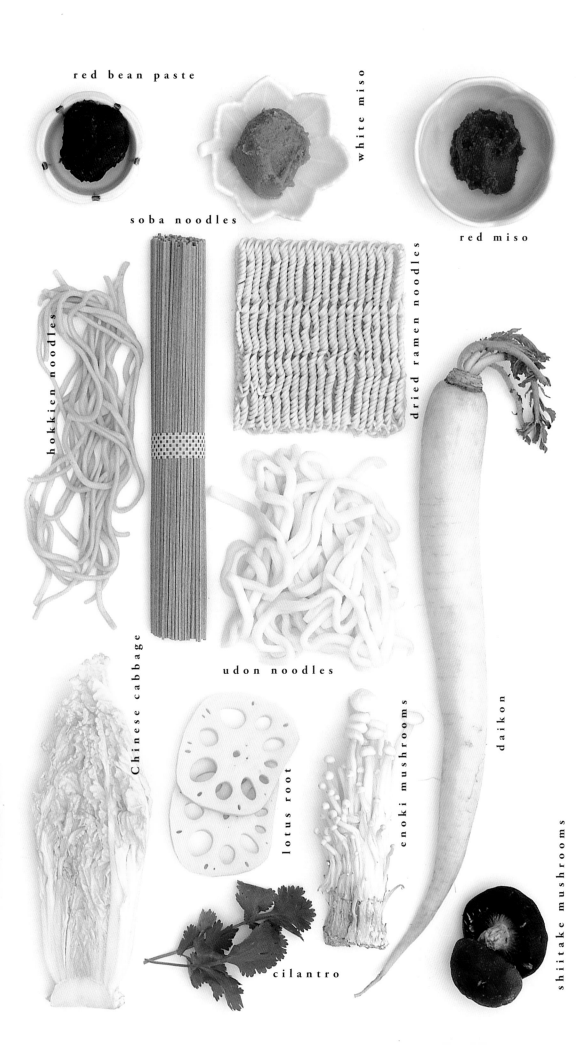

red bean paste

white miso

red miso

soba noodles

dried ramen noodles

hokkien noodles

daikon

udon noodles

Chinese cabbage

lotus root

enoki mushrooms

cilantro

shiitake mushrooms

Stock your shelves with nori, soba noodles, somen noodles, udon noodles, ramen noodles, kombu,

chili pepper, sesame oil, mustard, mirin, rice vinegar, wasabi, sake, chili oil, dashi sachets, soy sauce,

pickled ginger, sesame seeds, inari, red bean paste, wasabi, wakame, tempura flour, panko breadcrumbs,

Kewpie mayonnaise, tonkatsu, bonito flakes, tenkasu, rice, matcha, dashi granules, curry paste, ao nori

utensils

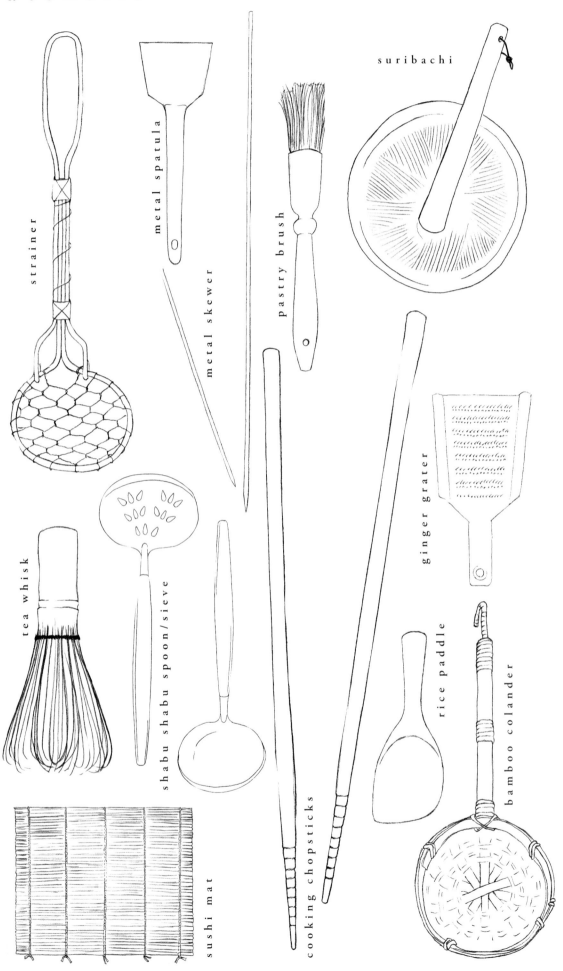

strainer

metal spatula

metal skewer

pastry brush

suribachi

tea whisk

shabu shabu spoon/sieve

ginger grater

cooking chopsticks

rice paddle

bamboo colander

sushi mat

how to cook rice

The easiest way to cook perfect rice every time is to buy a rice cooker – after all, millions of Chinese, Thai people and Japanese could not be wrong! If, however, you are a purist and you insist on cooking your rice on the stovetop, here is how it is done. It is much easier to cook rice on a gas stovetop rather than an electric one as the temperature is much easier to control. (This is why, if I am cooking on electric, I usually remove the rice once it forms tunnels and allow it to steam off the heat, which saves risking it sticking to the bottom.)

First you need to decide how much rice you want to cook. If you start off with 1 cup (250 mL) of uncooked rice remember that the cooking water will be absorbed and you will end up with approximately 3 cups (750 mL) of cooked rice. This means that about 1½ cups (375 mL) of uncooked rice is enough to serve 4 hungry people with a main meal.

Rinse the rice before you cook it to remove any grit. Put the drained, rinsed rice into a saucepan – make sure it is large enough to hold the cooked expanded volume of rice, as if the pan is too small the rice will not have room to move and will stick together. Add enough water to cover the rice (see below) and bring it to the boil. Boil, uncovered, until you see tunnels appear in the rice (which usually takes about 3–5 minutes). Turn the heat down as low as it will go if you have gas, cover the pan and cook for 10 minutes. Remove the rice from the heat and allow it to stand for 5 minutes before serving.

NOTE: A tried and tested way of measuring how much rice to water you need is to put the rice into a saucepan and pour in enough water to come up to your knuckle on your thumb when it is rested on the rice.

how to make sushi rice

1½ cups (375 mL) sushi rice

FOR THE DRESSING
2 tablespoons (30 mL) rice vinegar
1 tablespoon (15 mL) superfine sugar
2 teaspoons (10 mL) salt

Preparation time: 5 minutes, plus draining and cooling • Cooking time: 20 minutes • Makes 4 cups (1 L)

Wash the rice under cold running water until the water runs clear. Drain well.

Put the rice in a large saucepan, add 1½ cups (375 mL) water and bring to the boil. Boil for 5 minutes, or until tunnels appear in the surface.

Turn the heat down to low if you are using gas, otherwise take the pan off the heat. Cover and cook or leave to stand for 10 minutes, or until all the liquid has been absorbed and the rice is soft.

Put the dressing ingredients into another saucepan and stir over a low heat until the sugar dissolves.

Using a spatula, transfer the rice to a large flat tray and pour over the dressing. Use a sideways cutting motion to mix the dressing through the rice.

Cover with a damp tea towel and set aside to cool completely.

NOTE: Sushi rice only keeps for one day.

how to make sushi rolls

Making perfect sushi takes practice and patience, but is well worth the effort.
Serve with soy sauce and wasabi paste.

4–6 sheets roasted nori
2½ cups (625 mL) cooked seasoned sushi rice (see page 15)
2 tablespoons (30 mL) Kewpie mayonnaise
about 8–12 tempura prawns
1 avocado, cut into thin strips

Preparation time: 20 minutes • Cooking time: None if you have already cooked the rice •
Serves 4

PUT a sheet of nori onto a sushi mat.

SPREAD rice over two-thirds of the nori.

SPREAD a line of mayonnaise over the centre of
the rice.

TOP WITH 2–3 tempura prawns, depending on
size, and a strip of avocado.

ROLL THE nori over to the top edge of the rice,
tighten with the sushi mat and continue to roll.

CUT THE roll in half, then into thirds.
Repeat with remaining ingredients.

SUGGESTED FILLINGS FROM TOP:

Cucumber; Sashimi tuna; Sashimi salmon; Smoked salmon, chives, cream cheese and cucumber; Tempura vegetables – sweet potato, beans and red bell pepper; Tempura prawn, avocado and lettuce; Chicken teriyaki, mayonnaise and lettuce

how to make inside-out rolls

Spread the rice over the nori with damp fingertips and use the sushi mat to ensure that you have a tight roll. Serve with soy sauce and wasabi paste.

4 sheets roasted nori
2 cups (500 mL) cooked seasoned sushi rice (see page 15)
1 tablespoon (15 mL) wasabi paste or Kewpie mayonnaise
3 crabsticks
1 avocado, sliced
½ cucumber, cut into thin strips
¾ oz (20 g) flying fish roe

Preparation time: 30 minutes • Cooking time: None if you have already cooked the rice •
Makes 4

LAY A sheet of plastic wrap over a sushi mat.

PUT A sheet of nori onto the plastic wrap.

USE DAMP hands to cover the nori with the rice.

TURN OVER, smear wasabi along the center and top with crab, avocado and cucumber.

ROLL THE nori over to the edge of the filling and roll up, tightening the mat as you roll.

UNWRAP the roll and coat in the roe. Cut in half, then cut into thirds. Repeat.

Suggested fillings from top:

Tuna, mayonnaise and lettuce rolled in ao nori; Avocado, cream cheese and spring onion rolled in smoked salmon; Chicken katsu, lettuce and mayonnaise; Inari, pickled ginger and cucumber rolled in black sesame seeds; Tempura prawn, lettuce and mayonnaise rolled in sesame seeds; Crab, lettuce, mayonnaise and avocado rolled in flying fish roe

how to make hand rolls

Before rolling the hand rolls put a couple of grains of rice on the opposite edge
of the nori to seal and stop them unravelling.

10 sheets roasted nori
2 cups (500 mL) cooked seasoned sushi rice (see page 15)
10 oz (300 g) sashimi grade tuna fillet, skin removed and sliced
1 spring onion, finely sliced
½ teaspoon (2 mL) shichimi togarashi powder

Preparation time: 15 minutes • Cooking time: None if you have already cooked the rice •
Serves 4

Cut a nori sheet in half.

SHAPE 2 heaped tablespoons of rice
into a triangle.

Put the rice triangle on one end of nori and
flatten slightly.

Top with spring onion and tuna strips.
Sprinkle with the shichimi powder.

Roll the nori over to form a cone shape.

Seal and repeat with   rest of ingredients.

how to make nigiri

This is a simple way to make sushi. Keep your hands wet when shaping the rice
and using a tablespoon measure will ensure that the rice is all the same size.

2 cups (500 mL) cooked seasoned sushi rice (see page 15)
wasabi paste, to taste
1 x recipe tamago (see page 29)
½ sheet roasted nori, cut into small strips

*Preparation time: 20 minutes • Cooking time: None if you have already cooked the rice and
tamago • Makes 12*

SHAPE tablespoons of rice into ovals.

PUT the ovals on the work surface.

TOP EACH oval with a few dots of wasabi.

SLICE the tamago diagonally.

PUT the sliced tamago on top of the rice.

WRAP a strip of nori around the outside.

SUGGESTED FILLINGS FROM TOP:

Rare chargrilled beef, wasabi paste, watercress sprouts and shichimi togarashi powder; Boiled and butterflied prawn; Sliced tamago and nori; Marinated unagi (eel) and nori; Scallop and flying fish roe; Salmon tataki, mayonnaise and chives

how to make onigiri

These make a great snack or lunchtime meal. The rice can be shaped using a special mold or you can use damp hands to shape it into triangles instead.

2 cups (500 mL) cooked unseasoned sushi rice (see page 15)
4 umeboshi plums
½ sheet roasted nori or 2 tablespoons (30 mL) black sesame seeds

Preparation time: 30 minutes • Cooking time: None if you have already cooked the rice •
Makes 4

SHAPE tablespoons of rice into triangles.

PRESS your thumb into the centre.

FILL with umeboshi plums.

COVER the holes with rice.

CUT THE nori into strips, if using, about 1¼ inches (3 cm) wide and 6 inches (15cm) long.

WRAP the nori around the rice, or press the sides into sesame seeds and serve.

SUGGESTED FILLINGS FROM TOP:

Pickled vegetables wrapped in nori; Pickled ginger with edges crusted in sesame seeds;
Seaweed salad with strip of nori around the side; Ao nori filled with edamame; Umeboshi
with black sesame seeds; Flaked yakitori salmon with strip of nori

how to make gunkan/inari

Inari is a pouch of fried tofu usually filled with rice while gunkan maki, also called battleship sushi, is a special type of nigiri sushi (see page 22).

½ **sheet roasted nori**
5 sheets inari
2 cups (500 mL) cooked seasoned sushi rice (see page 15)
2 tablespoons (30 mL) toasted black sesame seeds

*Preparation time: 15 minutes • Cooking time: None if you have already cooked the rice •
Makes 10*

FOR GUNKAN, cut the nori into 6 equal strips.

FOR INARI SUSHI, cut the inari in half and cut a slit in the side to open into a pocket.

SHAPE tablespoons of the rice into mounds.

THREE-QUARTERS fill each pocket with the rice.

WRAP the rice in a strip of nori, seal with a grain of rice and top with your chosen topping.

FOLD the sides over to enclose and turn over to form a pocket.

SUGGESTED FILLINGS FROM TOP – these fillings can be mixed through the rice or put on top of the rice:

Black sesame and pickled ginger; Edamame; Pickled vegetables; Ao nori; Roasted nori; Black sesame seeds; Tuna mayonnaise (see page 25); Seaweed salad; Flying fish roe

h o w   t o   m a k e   d a s h i   s t o c k

1 piece (about 1 oz/30 g) kombu
¾ oz (20 g) bonito flakes

Preparation time: 5 minutes • Cooking time: 15 minutes • Makes 6 cups (1.5 liters)

Wipe the kombu clean using a damp piece of absorbent kitchen paper.

Cut the kombu several times – this will help to release its flavor into the stock.

Put the kombu and 4 cups (1 liter) of water into a saucepan and slowly bring to the boil over a low heat.

Remove the kombu as soon as the water comes to the boil – the kombu should be soft.

Add ¼ cup (60 mL) of water to the pan, add the bonito flakes, return to the boil once again, then as soon as it reaches boiling point remove from the heat.

Allow the flakes to settle to the bottom of the pan.
Strain through a sieve lined with absorbent kitchen paper.

NOTES: You can reuse the kombu and dashi to make another stock – this is known as secondary dashi, which is also used for noodles that are flavoured with other ingredients.
You can also make dashi by combining instant dashi granules, available from Asian food stores, with water – following the packet instructions for quantities. Be sure to check the packet carefully as a lot of these granules contain monosodium glutamate (MSG).

how to make tamago

6 eggs, lightly beaten
3 tablespoons (45 mL) dashi stock (see opposite)
1 tablespoon (15 mL) superfine sugar
2 teaspoons (10 mL) light soy sauce
2 tablespoons (30 mL) rice bran oil or vegetable oil, for oiling

Preparation time: 5 minutes: • Cooking time: 20 minutes • Serves 4

Lightly whisk the egg, dashi stock, sugar and soy sauce together in a bowl.

Heat a square Japanese omelette pan or a non-stick frying pan, brush generously with the oil and pour in enough egg mixture to cover the bottom of the pan. As it starts to cook the mixture will bubble up, so press it down with a soft spatula, then gently roll it towards you.

Push the rolled omelette to the other end of the pan and check to see if the pan needs to be oiled again. Pour in more of the egg mixture to cover the bottom, making sure it flows underneath the omelette you have just cooked.

Once the base is set, roll the cooked omelette back towards you again, picking up the new omelette as you go. Keep repeating this process until you have used up all the egg.

Wrap the omelette in a dry sushi mat and allow to cool. Slice and use in sushi rolls or use on top of rice or shredded in fried rice. The omelette may also be served on top of rice to make tamago nigiri sushi (see page 22) or it can be served as an accompaniment to meals or eaten on its own as a snack.

soups and starters

Japanese soups are often eaten as a main meal or as a snack in between meals, whether it be a simple miso that accompanies a meal or a large bowl of udon noodles in a light broth topped with a crisp tempura.

sashimi

7 oz (200 g) sashimi grade tuna fillet
7 oz (200 g) sashimi grade salmon fillet, skin removed
1 carrot, peeled
1 daikon, scrubbed
wasabi paste, to serve

FOR THE TOSA DIPPING SAUCE
3 tablespoons (45 mL) mirin
⅓ cup (80 mL) soy sauce

Cut the tuna and salmon into 6 x 3 inch (15 x 8 cm) rectangles using a sharp knife.

Slice the tuna and salmon rectangles into ¾ inch thick (2 cm) slices and arrange on a plate.

For the dipping sauce, put the mirin and soy sauce into a saucepan and boil over a high heat for 5 minutes to cook off the alcohol. Allow to cool.

Serve the dipping sauce and wasabi in small bowls on the side.

NOTES: You can serve the sashimi with a mound of finely grated carrot and daikon on the side. If you would like to make tataki, cook the tuna or salmon in a lightly oiled frying pan over a high heat for 30 seconds on each side or until the fish changes color. Allow to stand for 5 minutes before cutting into thin slices.

Preparation time: 5 minutes • Cooking time: 5 minutes • Serves 4

minced pepper pork ramen

3 tablespoons (45 mL) toasted sesame seeds
1 teaspoon (5 mL) sea salt
½ teaspoon (2 mL) cracked black pepper
1 tablespoon (15 mL) sunflower oil
1 clove garlic, crushed
14 oz (400 g) fatty ground pork
1 tablespoon (15 mL) chili paste
14 oz (400 g) dried ramen noodles
3½ oz (100 g) baby spinach leaves
6 cups (1.5 liters) chicken stock
3 spring onions, finely sliced
½ cup (125 mL) fresh cilantro sprigs
shichimi togarashi powder, to serve

Put the sesame seeds, salt and black pepper into a suribachi or mortar and pestle and grind lightly to break the seeds and combine. Don't be too vigorous or you will end up with a paste.

Heat the oil in a frying pan, add the garlic and pork and cook over a high heat for 5 minutes, or until the meat is browned. Add the sesame, salt and pepper mix and the chili paste and cook for a further 2 minutes, or until the pork is tender.

Cook the noodles in a large saucepan of boiling water until tender, then drain well. Divide the noodles among 4 serving bowls and top with the spinach. Bring the chicken stock to the boil in another saucepan and ladle over the noodles and spinach.

Top with the pork, spring onions and cilantro and serve with the shichimi togarashi powder on the side.

Preparation time: 15 minutes • Cooking time: 20 minutes • Serves 4

zaru soba

10 oz (300 g) dried soba noodles
2 sheets roasted nori, finely shredded
1 teaspoon (5 mL) wasabi powder made into a paste
2 spring onions, finely sliced
3 tablespoons (45 mL) finely grated daikon

FOR THE DIPPING SAUCE
2½ cups (625 mL) dashi stock (see page 28)
½ cup (125 mL) dark soy sauce
¼ cup (60 mL) mirin
3 tablespoons (45 mL) bonito flakes

To make the dipping sauce, put the stock, soy sauce and mirin into a saucepan and bring to the boil. Remove from the heat, add the bonito flakes and stir until the flakes are saturated. Strain and set aside to cool.

Cook the soba noodles in a large saucepan of boiling water until tender, then drain well and plunge into a bowl of iced water to stop them cooking. Set aside to cool in the iced water.

Drain the noodles and divide them among 4 serving baskets or bowls. Top with the shredded nori. Serve each person a pot of dipping sauce and condiment plates with wasabi, spring onions and daikon.

Preparation time: 5 minutes • Cooking time: 15 minutes • Serves 4

tempura

7 oz (200 g) sweet potato, peeled and cut into julienne
1 onion, thinly sliced
3½ oz (100 g) shiitake mushrooms
3½ oz (100 g) lotus root, sliced
1 red bell pepper, sliced
8 prawns, peeled and deveined with tails left intact
tempura flour or all-purpose flour, for dusting
vegetable oil, for deep-frying

FOR THE DIPPING SAUCE
¼ teaspoon (1 mL) dashi granules
⅓ cup (80 mL) mirin
⅓ cup (80 mL) light soy sauce

FOR THE TEMPURA BATTER
2 egg yolks
2 cups (500 mL) chilled soda water
2 cups (500 mL) tempura flour or all-purpose flour, sifted

To make the dipping sauce, heat the dashi granules, 2 tablespoons of water, the mirin and soy sauce in a saucepan until it boils. Allow to cool to room temperature.

To make the batter, whisk the egg yolks and chilled soda water together in a bowl. Add the sifted flour and, using chopsticks, stir until just combined. The batter should still be lumpy.

Dry the sweet potato, onion, shiitake mushrooms, sliced lotus, red bell pepper and prawns with absorbent kitchen paper and dust lightly with flour. Cut a star in the top of the shiitake mushrooms.

For the tempura vegetable discs, put the sweet potato and onion in a bowl. Add half the tempura batter and roughly mix to combine with a spoon.

Heat the oil for deep-frying in a large saucepan until it starts to move and bubble when a chopstick is stood up in it. Deep-fry ¼ cup (60 mL) of the sweet potato mixture until crisp and golden, then drain well.

For the prawn tempura, dip the prawns in the batter, allowing any excess to drain off and deep-fry until crisp and golden, then drain.

Dip the mushrooms, pepper and sliced lotus in the batter and deep-fry in batches until crisp and golden. Serve the tempura with the dipping sauce on the side.

NOTE: You can make other types of vegetable tempura by dipping your choice of vegetables in the batter until coated then deep-frying. Try using spinach leaves, shiso leaves and roasted nori.

Preparation time: 15 minutes • Cooking time: 15 minutes • Serves 4

Use chopsticks to mix the batter –
this helps to aerate the batter and
make the tempura crisp

PRAWN TEMPURA UDON

vegetable tempura udon

1 tablespoon (15 mL) wakame
14 oz (400 g) fresh or dried udon noodles
5 cups (1.25 liters) dashi stock (see page 28)
4 vegetable tempura discs (see page 38)
3 spring onions, finely sliced
shichimi togarashi powder

Soak the wakame in a bowl of warm water for 5 minutes, or until the leaves have expanded and are soft.

If using dried noodles, cook in a saucepan of boiling water for 5 minutes until tender. Drain well and divide among 4 serving bowls. If using fresh noodles, divide among the serving bowls.

Bring the dashi stock to the boil in a saucepan and ladle over the noodles. Top with a disc of vegetable tempura, some wakame and a handful of spring onions and sprinkle with the shichimi togarashi powder.

Preparation time: 20 minutes • Cooking time: 10 minutes, plus 5 minutes soaking • Serves 4

prawn tempura udon

1 tablespoon (15 mL) wakame
14 oz (400 g) fresh or dried udon noodles
6 cups (1.5 liters) dashi stock (see page 28)
4 tempura prawns (see page 38)
3 spring onions, finely sliced

Soak the wakame in a bowl of warm water for 5 minutes, or until the leaves have expanded and are soft.

If using dried noodles, cook in a saucepan of boiling water for 5 minutes until tender. Drain well and divide among 4 serving bowls. If using fresh noodles, divide among the serving bowls.

Bring the dashi stock to the boil in a saucepan and ladle over the noodles. Top with a tempura prawn, some wakame and a handful of sliced spring onions.

Preparation time: 20 minutes • Cooking time: 10 minutes, plus 5 minutes soaking • Serves 4

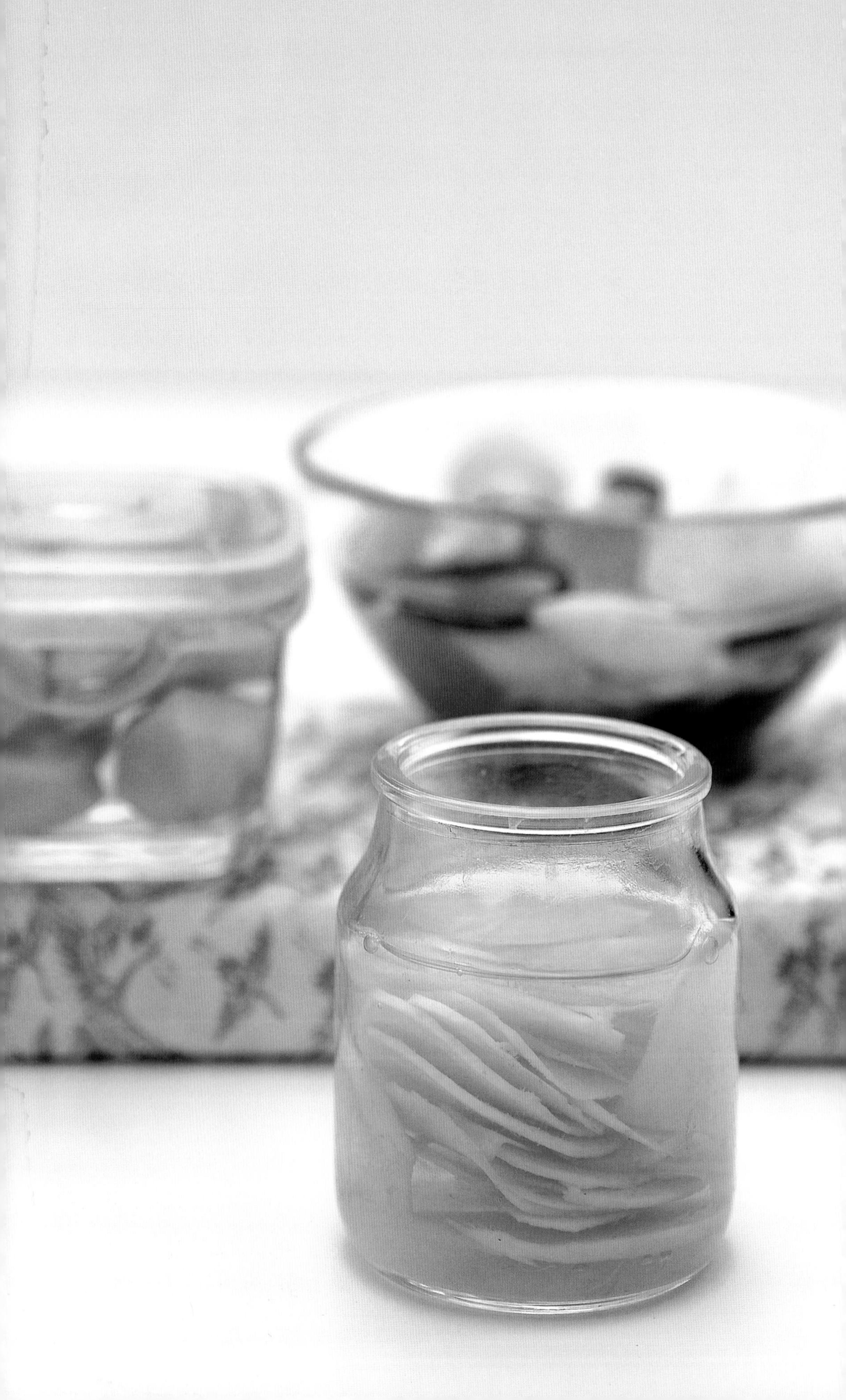

pickled vegetables

2 Lebanese cucumbers
2 carrots, peeled
1 daikon, scrubbed
4 cabbage leaves
8 oz (250 g) bean sprouts
3 tablespoons (45 mL) sea salt
2 teaspoons (10 mL) superfine sugar
2 cups (500 mL) rice vinegar

Cut the cucumbers in half lengthwise and scoop out the seeds, then cut the flesh into paper-thin slices. Cut the peeled carrot and daikon into thin slices and roughly chop the cabbage leaves. Remove the scraggly ends from the bean sprouts. Put the vegetables into 4 separate non-metallic bowls.

Sprinkle with salt and massage the salt into the vegetables. Allow to stand for 1 hour. Rinse and drain well. Put the vegetables into 1 large or 2 medium sterilized jars.

Put the sugar, rice vinegar and 1 cup (250 mL) of water into a saucepan, stir over a low heat until the sugar dissolves, then bring to the boil.

As soon as the sugar mixture boils, pour it over the vegetables, cover and allow to stand for 1–2 days before eating.

Preparation time: 10 minutes, plus 1 hour and 1–2 days standing • Cooking time: 5 minutes
• Makes 2 cups (500 mL)

pickled ginger

8 oz (250 g) fresh young ginger, peeled
2 teaspoons (10 mL) salt
1 cup (250 mL) rice vinegar
2 tablespoons (30 mL) superfine sugar

Rub the ginger clean using a damp cloth, then put on a plate and sprinkle with the salt. Allow to stand for 24 hours.

Put the rice vinegar, ½ cup (125 mL) of water and the sugar into a saucepan and stir over a low heat until the sugar dissolves. Pour into a sterilized jar.

Add the ginger to the jar, seal with a lid and allow to stand for 7 days – the ginger will turn pink on standing.

Cut the ginger into paper-thin slices and serve with sushi or your chosen dish.

Preparation time: 10 minutes, plus 8 days standing • Cooking time: None •
Makes 2 cups (500 mL)

gyoza

10 oz (300 g) ground pork or chicken
7 oz (200 g) peeled raw prawns, finely chopped
½ cup (125 mL) shredded Chinese cabbage
2 spring onions, sliced
2 teaspoons (10 mL) fresh grated ginger
1 egg, lightly beaten
2 teaspoons (10 mL) soy sauce
1 teaspoon (5 mL) mirin
1 teaspoon (5 mL) sake
30 gyoza wrappers, or as needed
2 tablespoons (30 mL) vegetable oil, for frying

FOR THE DIPPING SAUCE
3 tablespoons (45 mL) soy sauce
3 tablespoons (45 mL) rice vinegar
1½ teaspoons (7 mL) sesame oil
1½ teaspoons (7 mL) superfine sugar
pinch of chili flakes

Put the ground pork, prawns, shredded cabbage, spring onions, grated ginger, egg, soy sauce, mirin and sake into a bowl and mix to combine.

Lay a gyoza wrapper on a board and put 2 teaspoons (10 mL) of the filling in the center.

Brush the edges lightly with water, then bring the edges together to enclose the filling and press to seal. Repeat with the remaining wrappers.

Heat the oil in a large frying pan and add enough gyoza to cover the bottom of the pan. Cook until the bases of the gyoza are crisp and golden.

Add ½ cup (125 mL) of water, cover and cook for 5 minutes, or until all of the liquid has evaporated.

Mix the soy sauce, rice vinegar, sesame oil, sugar and chili flakes together in a bowl and serve with the gyoza.

Preparation time: 30 minutes • Cooking time: 15 minutes • Makes 30

cold tofu with ponzu dressing

10 oz (300 g) silken firm tofu
1 tablespoon (15 mL) finely shredded carrot
1 tablespoon (15 mL) finely shredded daikon
snow pea shoots, to serve

FOR THE PONZU DRESSING
2 tablespoons (30 mL) light soy sauce
1½ tablespoons (22 mL) lemon juice
1½ tablespoons (22 mL) mirin

To make the dressing, whisk together the soy sauce, lemon juice and mirin in a bowl.

Cut the tofu into large squares and arrange in 4 serving bowls.

Top each square of tofu with some shredded carrot and daikon, then pour the dressing over the top and finish with snow pea shoots.

NOTE: This dish is often served as a starter with yakitori.

Preparation time: 15 minutes • Cooking time: None • Serves 4

edamame

1 lb (500 g) fresh or frozen soy beans
sea salt flakes
dipping sauce of your choice, to serve

Cook the soy beans in a saucepan of boiling water until tender. Drain well and divide among 4 serving bowls.

Sprinkle with the sea salt and serve with your choice of dipping sauce.

NOTE: This dish is served in Japan with beer before meals or as a snack.

Preparation time: 2 minutes • Cooking time: 10 minutes • Serves 4

miso soup

3½ oz (100 g) silken firm tofu
1 tablespoon (15 mL) wakame
1 teaspoon (5 mL) dashi granules
3 tablespoons (45 mL) red miso
2 spring onions, finely sliced, to garnish

Cut the tofu into small cubes.

Soak the wakame in a bowl of warm water for 5 minutes, or until the leaves have expanded and are soft. Drain well.

Put 4 cups (1 liter) of water and the dashi granules into a saucepan, add the wakame and bring to the boil. Reduce the heat and allow to simmer for 10 minutes.

Blend the miso with a little of the hot stock and return to the pan, do not boil.

Divide the tofu among 4 serving bowls.

Pour over the hot stock and garnish with the spring onions.

Preparation time: 10 minutes, plus 5 minutes soaking • Cooking time: 15 minutes • Serves 4

chicken ramen

4 small skinless chicken breasts
½ teaspoon (2 mL) chili flakes
1 tablespoon (15 mL) soy sauce
1 tablespoon (15 mL) sake
1 tablespoon (15 mL) mirin
1 teaspoon (5 mL) superfine sugar
1 tablespoon (15 mL) sunflower oil, for oiling
7 oz (200 g) dried ramen noodles
1 tablespoon (15 mL) miso
6 cups (1.5 liters) chicken stock
7 oz (200 g) corn kernels
1¾ oz (50 g) fresh or pickled bean sprouts
fresh cilantro sprigs

Put the chicken into a shallow non-metallic bowl, add the chili flakes, soy sauce, sake, mirin and sugar and mix to coat the chicken. Cover and allow to marinate in the refrigerator for 30 minutes, or longer if time permits.

Cook the chicken on a lightly oiled barbecue or stovetop grill pan for about 15 minutes, or until golden brown and tender. Allow to stand for 10 minutes before cutting into thick slices.

Cook the noodles in a large saucepan of boiling water until tender, then drain well. Divide the noodles among 4 serving bowls.

Combine the miso with the chicken stock, then gently heat the mixture in another saucepan until it is just about to boil. Ladle over the noodles.

Top with the chicken, corn, bean sprouts and cilantro sprigs.

Preparation time: 20 minutes, plus 30 minutes marinating and 10 minutes standing •
Cooking time: 30 minutes • Serves 4

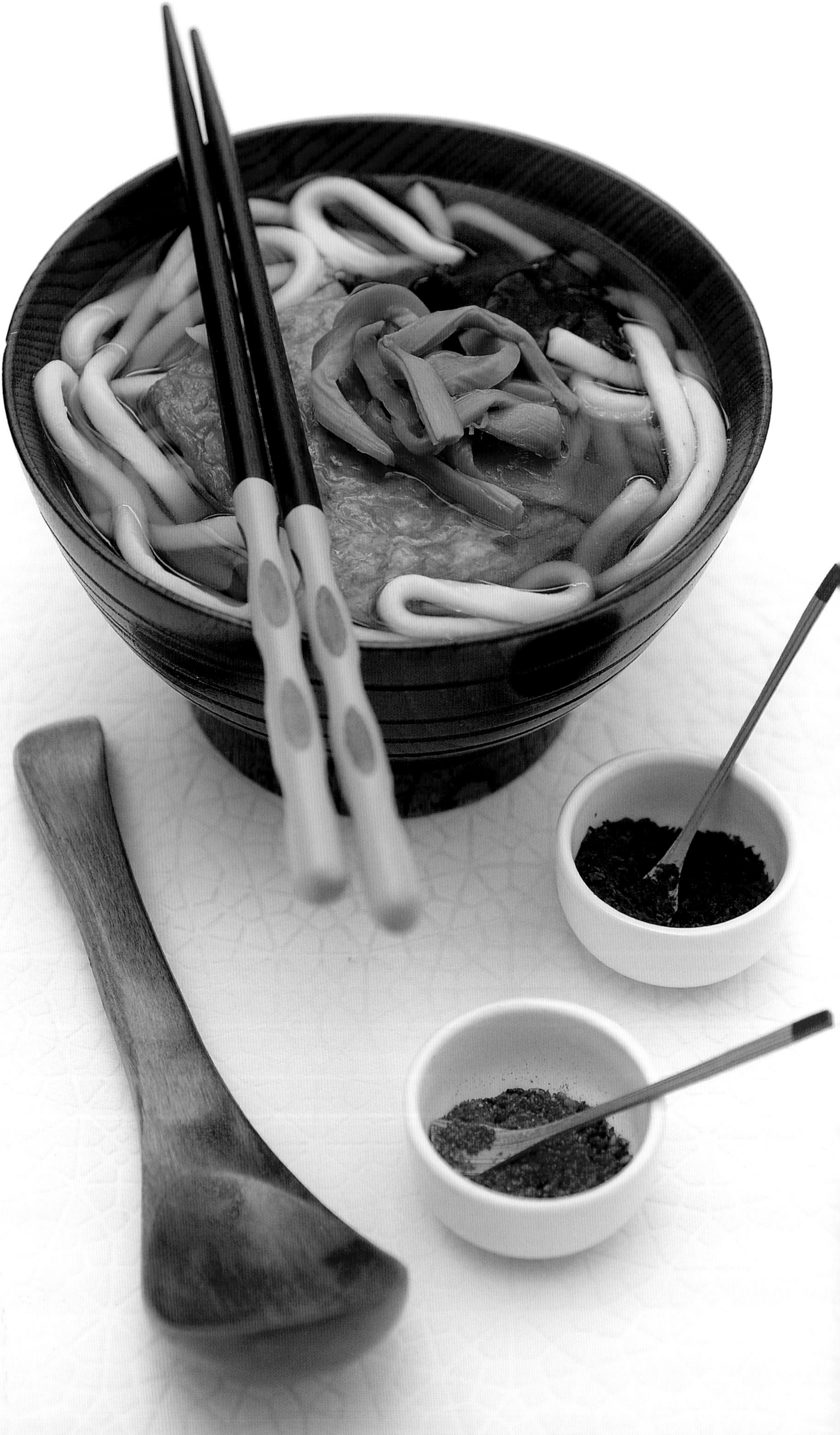

kitsune udon

1 tablespoon (15 mL) wakame
7 oz (200 g) fresh or dried udon noodles
4 cups (1 liter) dashi stock (see page 28)
4 x 4 inch (10 cm) squares inari
3 spring onions, finely sliced
16 pieces canned menma (pickled bamboo shoots)

TO SERVE (OPTIONAL)
ao nori
shichimi togarashi powder

Soak the wakame in a bowl of warm water for 5 minutes, or until the leaves have expanded and are soft. Drain well.

If using dried noodles, cook in a saucepan of boiling water for 5 minutes until tender. Drain well and divide among 4 serving bowls. If using fresh noodles, divide among the serving bowls.

Bring the dashi stock to the boil in a saucepan and ladle over the noodles. Top with a piece of inari, some wakame, a handful of spring onions and a spoonful of menma. Serve with ao nori and shichimi togarashi powder, if using.

Preparation time: 10 minutes, plus 5 minutes soaking • Cooking time: 10 minutes • Serves 4

glazed salmon soba

1 tablespoon (15 mL) sunflower oil
4 thin salmon fillets with skin on (about 4 oz/125 g each)
¼ cup (60 mL) soy sauce
3 tablespoons (45 mL) mirin
3 tablespoons (45 mL) sake
1½ tablespoons (22 mL) superfine sugar
7 oz (200 g) dried soba noodles
8 cups (2 liters) soy ramen broth
1¾ oz (50 g) enoki mushrooms
2 hard-boiled eggs, peeled and halved
1¾ oz (50 g) bok choy, separated into leaves

Heat the oil in a frying pan, add the salmon and cook over a medium heat for 5–7 minutes, or until golden brown on both sides. Remove from the pan. Add the soy sauce, mirin, sake and sugar and stir over a low heat until the sugar dissolves. Bring to the boil and cook over a high heat until the sauce thickens and reduces slightly.

Add the salmon back to the pan and cook until the salmon is glazed and cooked to your liking. Remove from the heat.

Cook the noodles in a large saucepan of boiling water until tender, then drain well. Divide among 4 serving bowls.

Bring the ramen broth to the boil in another saucepan, then ladle over the noodles and top with the salmon, mushroom, egg and bok choy.

Preparation time: 20 minutes • Cooking time: 20 minutes • Serves 4

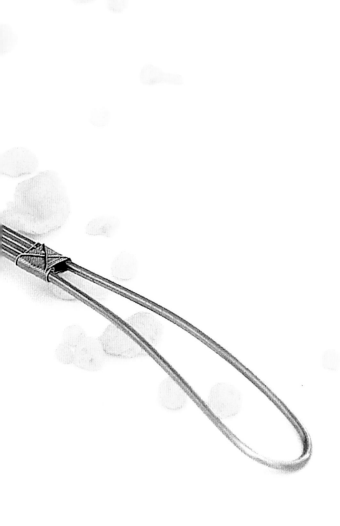

grilled and fried

Sticky, sweet and salty yakitori, crisp, golden deep-fried tofu and sizzling teppanyaki
plates – these are all cornerstones of Japanese cuisine and can be served as part of a meal or
as a meal in themselves.

yakitori salmon

1 lb (500 g) salmon fillet with skin on
sea salt flakes
3 tablespoons (45 mL) soy sauce
1 tablespoon (15 mL) mirin
1 tablespoon (15 mL) sake
2 teaspoons (10 mL) superfine sugar
lemon wedges, to serve

Cut the salmon into 1¼ inch thick (3 cm) strips and put onto a non-metallic plate. Sprinkle all over with the salt and allow to stand for 30 minutes. Rinse and pat dry with absorbent kitchen paper. Preheat a grill or light a barbecue or hibachi (traditional Japanese barbecue).

Put the soy sauce, mirin, sake and sugar into a saucepan and stir over a low heat until the sugar dissolves, then bring to the boil and cook until the sauce thickens slightly.

Thread the salmon on 3 parallel metal skewers, then repeat with the remaining salmon using 3 more metal skewers and cook over the hot barbecue or under the grill until tender.

Brush the salmon lightly on both sides with the sauce and serve with lemon wedges.

Preparation time: 5 minutes, plus 30 minutes standing • Cooking time: 5–10 minutes • Serves 4

yakiudon

14 oz (400 g) fresh or dried udon noodles
2 tablespoons (30 mL) soy sauce
2 tablespoons (30 mL) tonkatsu sauce
1 teaspoon (5 mL) superfine sugar
½ teaspoon (2 mL) chili flakes
14 oz (400 g) chicken thigh fillets, chopped
1 tablespoon (15 mL) sunflower oil
1 red bell pepper, sliced
3½ oz (100 g) shiitake mushrooms
1 bunch bok choy or pak choi, roughly chopped

Gently separate the noodles and set aside.

Combine the soy sauce, tonkatsu sauce, sugar and chili flakes in a large non-metallic bowl, add the chicken and mix to coat in the marinade. Cover and allow to stand for 5–10 minutes, then drain the chicken, reserving the marinade to use as the sauce.

Heat the sunflower oil in a wok until it is smoking, add the chicken and cook over a high heat for about 10 minutes, or until the chicken is tender.

Add the bell pepper and mushrooms and stir-fry for 3 minutes, or until soft.

Add the noodles, reserved marinade and bok choy or pak choi and stir-fry for 2 minutes, or until heated through.

Preparation time: 15 minutes, plus 5–10 minutes standing • Cooking time: 15 minutes
• Serves 4

agedashi tofu

1¼ lb (600 g) silken firm tofu
potato starch or cornstarch, for dusting
1 tablespoon (15 mL) sake
2 tablespoons (30 mL) light soy sauce
2 tablespoons (30 mL) mirin
2 cups (500 mL) dashi stock (see page 28)
vegetable oil, for deep-frying
½ cup (125 mL) finely grated daikon
3 tablespoons bonito flakes
1 spring onion, finely sliced

Put the tofu between 2 sheets of absorbent kitchen paper in between 2 chopping boards weighted down to remove any excess moisture and allow to drain for 30 minutes.

Cut the tofu into blocks and roll in the potato starch or cornstarch until coated, shaking off any excess.

Put the sake, soy sauce, mirin and dashi stock into a saucepan, bring to the boil and cook over a high heat for 3 minutes to cook off the alcohol. Reduce the heat and keep at a low simmer while you cook the tofu.

Heat the oil in a large deep saucepan until it starts to move and bubble when a chopstick is stood up in it. Deep-fry the tofu in batches until crisp and golden and heated through, then drain on absorbent kitchen paper.

Divide the tofu among serving bowls, top with a small mound of daikon, bonito flakes and spring onion. Ladle the broth around the tofu and serve immediately.

Preparation time: 20 minutes, plus 30 minutes draining • Cooking time: 20 minutes • Serves 4

chicken karage

1 lb (500 g) skinless chicken thighs
1 tablespoon (15 mL) finely grated fresh ginger
2 tablespoons (30 mL) soy sauce
1 tablespoon (15 mL) sake
1 tablespoon (15 mL) mirin
½ cup (125 mL) potato starch or cornstarch
1 sheet roasted nori, cut into ¾ inch wide (2 cm) strips
sunflower or vegetable oil, for deep-frying
gyoza dipping sauce (see page 46) or choice of dipping sauce, to serve

Cut the chicken into bite-sized pieces and put into a non-metallic shallow dish. Add the ginger, soy sauce, sake and mirin and mix well to coat the chicken. Cover and allow to marinate overnight if time permits. Drain well.

Mix together the potato starch or cornstarch and nori on a large plate then use to coat the chicken in the mixture, shaking off any excess.

Heat the oil in a wok until it starts to move and bubble when a chopstick is stood up in it. Deep-fry the chicken in batches for 3–5 minutes, or until crisp, golden brown and cooked through. Drain on absorbent kitchen paper and keep warm while you cook the remaining chicken. Serve with gyoza dipping sauce or your choice of dipping sauce.

Preparation time: 15 minutes, plus 8 hours marinating • Cooking time: 15 minutes • Serves 4 as part of a meal

chicken and spring onion yakitori

4 skinless chicken thighs, cut into ¾ inch (2 cm) cubes
8 spring onions, cut into 1½ inch (4 cm) lengths
¼ cup (60 mL) sake
¼ cup (60 mL) mirin
½ cup (125 mL) soy sauce
½ teaspoon (2 mL) chili paste
1 teaspoon (5 mL) superfine sugar
1 tablespoon (15 mL) lemon juice

Soak 12 bamboo skewers in a bowl of cold water for 15 minutes to prevent burning during cooking.

Thread the chicken and spring onions onto the soaked skewers.

Combine the sake, mirin, soy sauce, chili paste, sugar and lemon in a large non-metallic dish, add the skewers and marinate for 4 hours, or overnight if time permits.

Preheat a grill or light a barbecue or hibachi (traditional Japanese barbecue) and cook the skewers for 20 minutes, or until tender.

Preparation time: 20 minutes, plus 15 minutes soaking and 4–8 hours marinating • Cooking time: 20 minutes • Serves 4

fried rice

2 tablespoons (30 mL) sunflower or vegetable oil
2 eggs, lightly beaten
1 tablespoon (15 mL) grated fresh ginger
10 oz (300 g) skinless chicken thigh fillets, chopped
3½ oz (100 g) enoki mushrooms
1 cup (250 mL) fresh or frozen peas
3 cups (750 mL) cold cooked rice
¼ cup (60 mL) chicken stock
1 tablespoon (15 mL) soy sauce
1 tablespoon (15 mL) mirin

Heat half the oil in a frying pan, add the beaten eggs and swirl to coat the bottom of
the pan. Cook over a medium heat for 3 minutes until set, lifting the edges to allow the
uncooked egg to run underneath. Turn over and cook the other side. Remove from the
pan and allow to cool for 5 minutes, then finely shred and set aside.

Heat the remaining oil in a wok until it is smoking, add the ginger and chicken and cook
over a high heat for 5 minutes, or until the chicken is browned and tender.

Add the mushrooms and peas and cook for a further 1 minute. Add the rice, shredded omelette, stock, soy sauce and mirin and cook, stirring, until the rice is heated through.

Preparation time: 15 minutes • Cooking time: 15 minutes • Serves 4

korokke

10 oz (300 g) starchy potatoes, peeled
1 tablespoon (15 mL) vegetable oil, plus extra for shallow-frying
1 onion, finely chopped
7 oz (200 g) ground pork or beef
1 teaspoon (5 mL) mustard powder
1 cup (250 mL) shredded Chinese cabbage
1 carrot, grated
sea salt
½ teaspoon (2 mL) white pepper
1 cup (250 mL) all-purpose flour
2 eggs, lightly beaten
1 cup (250 mL) panko breadcrumbs
salad and ketchup, to serve

Steam or boil the potatoes until soft. Mash the potato until smooth and set aside.

Heat the vegetable oil in a frying pan, add the onion and cook over a medium heat for
5 minutes, or until golden. Add the ground meat and mustard powder and cook for about
5 minutes, or until the meat is browned.

Add the cabbage and carrot and cook for a further 3 minutes, or until soft.

Put the mashed potato into a bowl with the meat mixture and season with sea salt and the
pepper. Divide the mixture into 4–6 equal portions and shape each portion into patties.

Coat the patties first in the flour, shaking off any excess, then dip in the lightly beaten egg
and finally in the breadcrumbs until coated.

Heat the oil for shallow-frying in a large deep frying pan until it starts to move then cook
the patties in batches for 3–5 minutes on each side, or until crisp and golden. Drain on
absorbent kitchen paper. Serve with salad and ketchup.

Preparation time: 15 minutes • Cooking time: 30 minutes • Serves 4–6

okonomiyaki

1 cup (250 mL) dashi stock (see page 28)
1 egg, lightly beaten
2 cups (500 mL) all-purpose flour
1 teaspoon (5 mL) baking powder
½ cup (125 mL) tenkasu
2 cups (500 mL) finely shredded Chinese cabbage
⅓ cup (80 mL) dried shrimp
2 tablespoons (30 mL) sunflower or vegetable oil
8 paper-thin slices pork belly

TO FINISH
tonkatsu sauce
Kewpie mayonnaise
bonito flakes
ao nori

Combine the dashi stock and egg in a bowl. Sift the flour and baking powder into a large bowl, add the dashi stock mixture and mix until smooth.

Add the tenkasu, cabbage and dried shrimp and mix to combine.

Heat a little of the oil in a lightly oiled stovetop grill pan or in a large frying pan, add 1 cup (250 mL) of the mixture and form into a pancake shape. Cook over a medium heat for 3–5 minutes, or until the base is crisp and golden brown.

Lay 2 of the pork slices over the top of the mixture, then spoon 2 tablespoons of the batter over the pork and spread to cover the top.

Turn over with a spatula and make 2 cuts in the top of the pancake (this helps the batter to cook all the way through and stops the pancake from becoming soggy). Cook over a low-medium heat until the base is crisp and golden and the pancake is cooked through. Keep warm while you cook the remaining batter.

Brush the top of the pancakes with tonkatsu sauce and zigzag the mayonnaise over the top. Sprinkle with the bonito flakes and shake the ao nori over the top. Cut into wedges and serve immediately.

Preparation time: 25 minutes • Cooking time: 40 minutes • Makes 4 pancakes

OKONOMIYAKI

The secret to a perfect pancake is to cook it over a medium heat and to test the center with a skewer to ensure it is cooked all the way through

chicken teriyaki

4 chicken breasts or thigh fillets with skin on
1 tablespoon (15 mL) sunflower oil
½ cup (125 mL) sake
½ cup (125 mL) mirin
½ cup (125 mL) soy sauce
1 tablespoon (15 mL) superfine sugar
freshly cooked snow peas, to serve

Pat the chicken dry with absorbent kitchen paper and pierce the skin several times with a skewer (this helps to release the fat from the skin and will enable it to crisp). Heat the sunflower oil in a frying pan, add the chicken and cook skin side down over a medium heat for 15–20 minutes, or until crisp and golden. Turn over, cover with a lid and cook for a further 10 minutes. Remove the chicken from the pan and set aside.

Add the sake, mirin, soy sauce and sugar to the frying pan and cook, stirring constantly, until the sugar dissolves. Bring to the boil and cook for 5 minutes, or until the sauce thickens and has a nice sheen.

Return the chicken to the pan and cook for a further 5 minutes, or until the chicken is coated in the sauce.

Preparation time: 10 minutes • Cooking time: 40 minutes • Serves 4

yakitori squid with mayonnaise and chili sprinkle

1 large fresh prepared squid or 1 squid tube with tentacles
sunflower or vegetable oil
1 tablespoon (15 mL) Kewpie mayonnaise
shichimi togarashi powder

Light a barbecue or hibachi (traditional Japanese barbecue). Clean the squid tube, reserving the tentacles and brush the squid tube and tentacles with the oil.

Cook the squid and tentacles over the barbecue for 2–3 minutes, or until white and tender.

Cut the squid into thick slices and serve on a long flat plate with a mound of mayonnaise and sprinkled with the shichimi togarashi powder.

Preparation time: 10 minutes • Cooking time: 5 minutes • Serves 4 as part of a meal

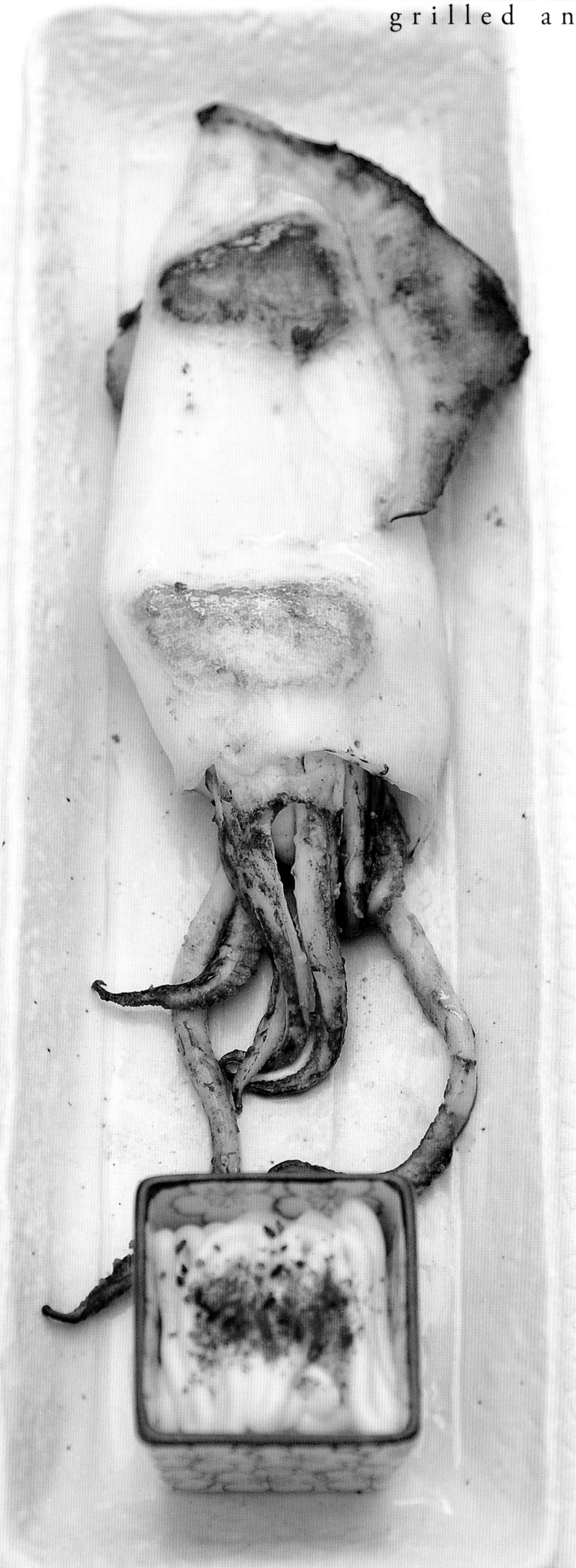

yakisoba

14 oz (400 g) hokkien noodles
1 tablespoon (15 mL) sunflower or vegetable oil
3 spring onions, thinly sliced
2 cloves garlic, chopped
1 tablespoon (15 mL) grated fresh ginger
14 oz (400 g) green prawns, peeled and roughly chopped, or skinless chicken thigh fillets,
  roughly chopped
1 carrot, cut into thin strips
4 cabbage leaves, roughly chopped
2 tablespoons (30 mL) light soy sauce
2 tablespoons (30 mL) tomato ketchup
2 tablespoons (30 mL) tonkatsu sauce
3½ oz (100 g) bean sprouts

TO SERVE
2 tablespoons (30 mL) pink pickled ginger
2 tablespoons (30 mL) toasted sesame seeds

Separate the noodles and set aside. Heat the oil in a wok until it is smoking then add the
spring onions, garlic and ginger and cook until the spring onions are soft.

Add the prawns and cook for 5 minutes, or until they turn pink. If using chicken, cook for
10 minutes, or until the chicken is browned and tender. Add the carrot and cabbage and
stir-fry for 3 minutes, or until they soften.

Add the noodles, soy sauce, ketchup and tonkatsu sauce and cook until the noodles are
coated with the sauce. Toss in the bean sprouts and remove from the heat.

Serve bowls of the noodles topped with the pickled ginger and sesame seeds.

Preparation time: 10 minutes • Cooking time: 15 minutes • Serves 4

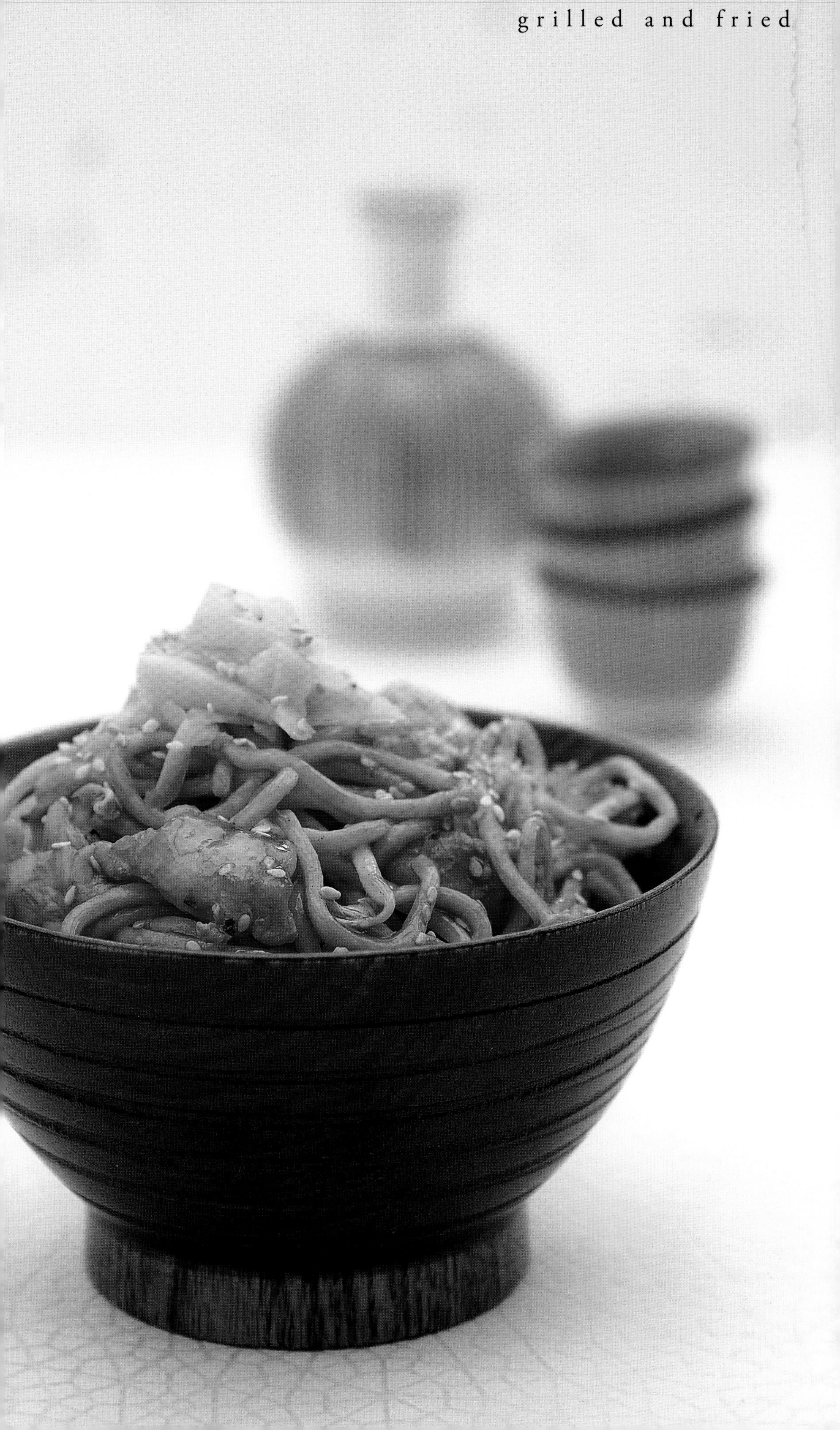

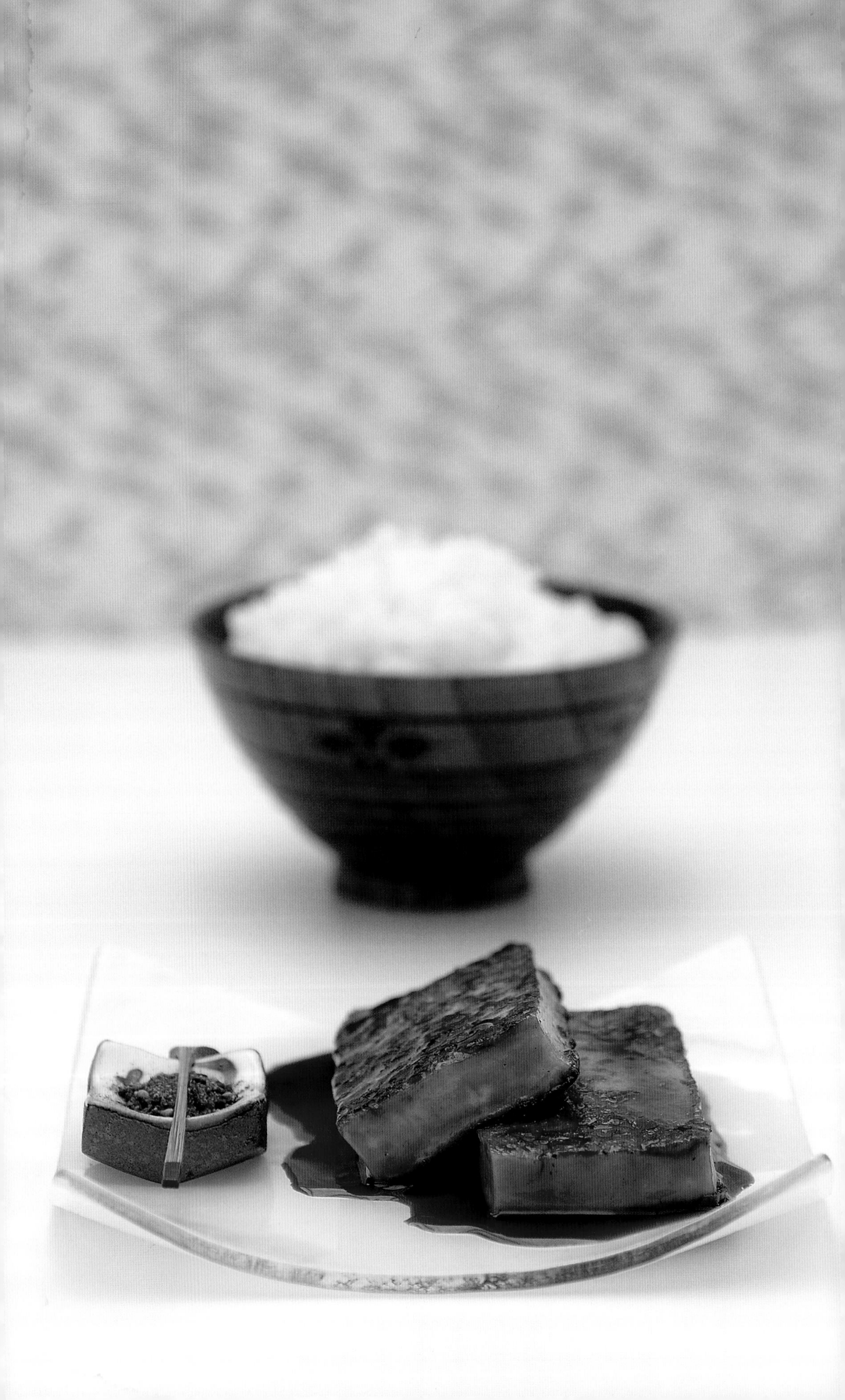

tofu teppanyaki

1 lb (500 g) silken firm tofu, drained
1½ tablespoons (22 mL) sunflower oil
3 tablespoons (45 mL) soy sauce
1 tablespoon (15 mL) mirin
1 tablespoon (15 mL) sake
1 tablespoon (15 mL) superfine sugar
2 spring onions, finely sliced (optional)
½ teaspoon shichimi togarashi powder
freshly cooked rice, to serve

Put the tofu onto a chopping board in between several layers of absorbent kitchen paper.
Top with another chopping board and weight down lightly. Allow to stand for 30 minutes
to remove any excess liquid. Cut into thick slices.

Heat the oil on a teppanyaki plate or a frying pan, add the tofu and cook until golden brown
on all sides. Remove.

Mix together the soy sauce, mirin, sake and sugar, then pour onto the plate or in the frying
pan and stir over a low heat until the sugar dissolves. Bring to the boil and cook for about
5 minutes, or until the sauce reduces and thickens slightly. Return the tofu to the plate
or frying pan and heat through quickly. Sprinkle with the spring onions, if using, and the
shichimi togarashi powder and serve with rice.

Preparation time: 15 minutes, plus 30 minutes standing • Cooking time: 15 minutes
• Serves 2–4

japanese hamburgers

½ cup (125 mL) panko breadcrumbs
½ cup (125 mL) milk
14 oz (400 g) ground beef
3½oz (100 g) ground pork
3 spring onions, finely sliced
1 egg, lightly beaten
¼ teaspoon (1 mL) wasabi powder
salad, to serve

FOR THE TERIYAKI SAUCE
½ cup (125 mL) mirin
½ cup (125 mL) sake
½ cup (125 mL) soy sauce
3 tablespoons (45 mL) superfine sugar

Put the breadcrumbs into a bowl, cover with the milk and allow to stand for 15 minutes, or until all the milk has been absorbed.

Put the ground beef and pork into a large bowl, add the spring onions, egg, wasabi and soaked breadcrumbs and, using your hands, mix well to combine. Divide the mixture into 8 equal portions and shape into hamburger patties, then cover with plastic wrap and allow to chill in the refrigerator for 30 minutes. Return to room temperature before cooking. Preheat the oven to 400°F (200°C).

Heat the oil on a barbecue flat plate or in a large frying pan, add the burgers in batches and cook for about 10 minutes, or until both sides are browned. Transfer to a baking tray and finish cooking in the oven for 10 minutes, or until cooked through.

Meanwhile, to make the teriyaki sauce, put the mirin, sake, soy sauce and sugar in a saucepan and stir over a low heat until the sugar dissolves. Bring to the boil and cook over a high heat for about 5 minutes, or until the sauce has reduced and thickened slightly.

Serve the burgers with salad and the teriyaki sauce.

Preparation time: 15 minutes, plus 15 minutes soaking and 30 minutes chilling • Cooking time: 30 minutes • Serves 4–8

grilled and fried

yakitori chicken meatballs threaded onto skewers

13 oz (375 g) skinless chicken thigh fillets
2 eggs, lightly beaten
½ teaspoon (2 mL) salt
1 tablespoon (15 mL) cornstarch
1 cup (250 mL) dried panko breadcrumbs
1 tablespoon (15 mL) grated fresh ginger
sunflower or vegetable oil, for oiling

FOR THE YAKITORI SAUCE
⅓ cup (80 mL) sake
⅓ cup + 1 tablespoon (100 mL) soy sauce
1 tablespoon (15 mL) mirin
1 tablespoon (15 mL) superfine sugar
½ teaspoon (2 mL) cornstarch blended with 1 teaspoon (5 mL) water

Roughly chop the chicken, then put into a food processor and process until finely ground.

Transfer the ground chicken to a large bowl, add the beaten egg, salt, cornstarch, bread-crumbs and ginger and, using your hands, mix well to combine.

Shape tablespoons of the mixture into balls and put on a plate. Cover and allow to chill in the refrigerator for 30 minutes, or until firm. Meanwhile, soak 8 bamboo skewers in cold water for 15 minutes to prevent burning during cooking. Preheat a grill or light a barbecue or hibachi (traditional Japanese barbecue).

Thread the balls onto the soaked skewers and brush lightly with oil. Cook under the grill or on the barbecue, turning several times until golden and tender.

For the sauce, put the sake, soy sauce, mirin and sugar in a saucepan and stir over a low heat until the sugar dissolves. Bring to the boil, then remove from the heat and stir in the corn-starch paste. Return to the heat and cook, stirring constantly, for about 5 minutes, or until the sauce boils and thickens.

Dip the chicken skewers into the sauce and serve.

Preparation time: 20 minutes, plus 30 minutes chilling • Cooking time: 20 minutes • Serves 4

tonkatsu

4 thick pork loin cutlets or steaks (boneless)
1 cup (250 mL) all-purpose flour seasoned with salt and pepper, for dusting
2 eggs, lightly beaten
2 cups (500 mL) panko breadcrumbs
vegetable oil, for shallow-frying

TO SERVE
tonkatsu sauce
Japanese mustard
freshly cooked rice and cabbage

Cut 3–4 slits in the fat on the side of the pork cutlets or steaks (this will stop them curling up as they cook).

Use a mallet to flatten each cutlet, then press to coat in the seasoned flour and dip in the beaten egg.

Coat the pork cutlets in the breadcrumbs and press to ensure they stick to the cutlets. Allow to stand for 30 minutes if time permits as this will help the crumbs hold.

Heat the vegetable oil for shallow-frying in a deep frying pan until it starts to move. Gently lower the cutlets in batches into the pan and cook over a medium heat for 5 minutes on each side, or until crisp, golden brown and cooked through. Drain on absorbent kitchen paper and keep warm while you cook the remaining cutlets. Serve with tonkatsu sauce and Japanese mustard, rice and cabbage.

NOTES: Tonkatsu is often served sliced on a Japanese curry sauce or sliced, cooked and served over rice. Chicken katsu is similar to this dish, but chicken is used instead of pork.

Preparation time: 20 minutes, plus 30 minutes standing • Cooking time: 20 minutes • Serves 4

cod in miso

2 tablespoons (30 mL) sake
¼ cup (60 mL) mirin
1 cup (250 mL) white miso
¾ cup (185 mL) superfine sugar
4 x 7 oz (200 g) cod fillets

FOR THE MASHED POTATO
4 potatoes, peeled and chopped
3½ oz (100 g) butter
½ cup (125 mL) milk
2 teaspoons (10 mL) wasabi paste

Put the sake and mirin into a small saucepan, bring to the boil and cook over a high heat for 2 minutes to cook off the alcohol. Add the miso and cook, stirring, until the miso softens.

Add the sugar and cook, stirring, until the sugar dissolves. Remove and allow to cool for 20 minutes.

Put the cod and miso mixture into an earthenware pot and mix to coat, then cover and allow to marinate in the refrigerator for 2 days.

Preheat the oven to 400°F (200°C) and preheat the broiler. Wipe any excess miso from the fish, keeping the marinade in the pot, and put the fish onto a baking tray. Cook under the broiler for 5 minutes, or until browned.

Put the fish back into the pot and bake in the oven for a further 10 minutes, or until tender.

Meanwhile, to make the mashed potatoes, cook the potatoes in a large saucepan of boiling water until tender, then drain and return to the pan. Add the butter, milk and wasabi and beat with electric beaters until smooth. Serve the miso cod with the wasabi mash.

Preparation time: 20 minutes, plus 2 days marinating • Cooking time: 20 minutes • Serves 4

If you don't have an earthenware pot then
use a baking dish or an ovenproof casserole
dish instead

COD IN MISO

salads

Salads are easy to make and can be served either warm and cold, eaten at home or taken to work in a handy bento box. Try a soba noodle and edamame salad splashed with a simple soy dressing or a seared tuna salad dressed with a sweet soy dressing.

sashimi salmon salad

1 lb (500 g) sashimi grade salmon fillet, finely chopped
1 avocado, finely chopped
1 oz (30 g) salmon roe
2 spring onions, finely sliced
2 teaspoons (10 mL) Kewpie mayonnaise
3½ oz (100 g) watercress sprouts, to serve

FOR THE DRESSING
2 tablespoons (30 mL) soy sauce
2 tablespoons (30 mL) lemon juice
1 teaspoon (5 mL) sesame oil
1 tablespoon (15 mL) bonito flakes

Whisk together the dressing ingredients to combine. Put the salmon and the dressing into a bowl, mix to coat, then allow to stand for 10 minutes.

Add the avocado, salmon roe, spring onions and mayonnaise to the bowl and mix gently to combine. Serve in bowls with the watercress sprouts.

NOTE: This salad is great served in hand rolls or in gunkan sushi (see pages 20–1 and 26–7).

Preparation time: 15 minutes, plus 10 minutes standing • Cooking time: None • Serves 4

eggplant and spring onion salad

8 baby Japanese eggplants
1 tablespoon (15 mL) finely grated fresh ginger
⅓ cup + 1 tablespoon (100 mL) soy sauce
2 tablespoons (30 mL) mirin
2 tablespoons (30 mL) sake
1 tablespoon (15 mL) rice vinegar
2 teaspoons (10 mL) sesame oil
2 teaspoons (10 mL) superfine sugar
3 tablespoons (45 mL) bonito flakes
1 spring onion, thinly sliced

Peel a thin strip of the skin off the eggplants to give a striped look, then cut the eggplants in half lengthwise.

Soak the eggplant pieces in a bowl of cold water for 10 minutes.

Arrange the eggplant on a plate in a bamboo steamer set over a wok of simmering water. Cover and steam for 10 minutes, or until the eggplant is tender. Drain well.

Put the ginger, soy sauce, mirin and sake into a saucepan, bring to the boil and cook off the alcohol for 3 minutes. Remove from the heat, then add the rice vinegar, sesame oil and sugar.

Arrange the eggplant on a serving plate, pour the dressing over the top and sprinkle with the bonito flakes and spring onion slices.

Preparation time: 15 minutes, plus 10 minutes soaking • Cooking time: 20 minutes • Serves 4 as a side salad

summer sesame chicken salad

3 Lebanese cucumbers
sea salt
14 oz (400 g) skinless chicken breast or thigh fillets
1 tablespoon (15 mL) sunflower oil
3½ oz (100 g) bean sprouts
4 spring onions, sliced
¼ cup (60 mL) fresh cilantro leaves

FOR THE SESAME SAUCE
6 tablespoons (90 mL) sesame seeds
2 tablespoons (30 mL) soy sauce
2 tablespoons (30 mL) mirin
1 tablespoon (15 mL) superfine sugar
½ tablespoon (7 mL) rice vinegar
1–2 teaspoons (5–10 mL) chili paste

Cut the cucumber into quarters lengthwise and put on a plate. Sprinkle with salt and allow to stand for 30 minutes. Rinse and pat dry with absorbent kitchen paper.

Brush the chicken lightly with the oil. Cook the chicken fillets in a stovetop grill pan for about 20 minutes, or until tender and golden brown. Allow to cool slightly before tearing into thin strips.

Arrange the cucumber and bean sprouts on a plate and top with the chicken.

To make the sauce, toast the sesame seeds in a frying pan. Transfer to a suribachi or mortar and pestle and grind to roughly crush the seeds. Remove half the seeds and set aside, then continue grinding the remaining seeds to form a paste.

Transfer the paste to a jug and add ¼ cup (60 mL) of water, the soy sauce, mirin, sugar, rice vinegar and chili paste. Transfer the mixture to a saucepan, bring to the boil and cook over a high heat for 3 minutes, then reduce the heat and allow to simmer for about 5 minutes until the sauce thickens slightly. If it is too thick, add 2 tablespoons (30 mL) of water to dilute.

Pour the warm sesame sauce over the chicken and top with the spring onions, cilantro and remaining sesame seeds.

Preparation time: 20 minutes, plus 30 minutes standing • Cooking time: 30–35 minutes
• Serves 4

chargrilled shiitake mushroom salad
topped with a ponzu dressing

12 large fresh shiitake mushrooms
3 spring onions, cut into short pieces
sea salt
1 tablespoon (15 mL) sunflower oil, for oiling
1 head baby romaine or butter lettuce

FOR THE PONZU DRESSING
2 tablespoons (30 mL) lemon juice
2 tablespoons (30 mL) soy sauce
½ tablespoon (7 mL) mirin

Cut a star in the top of each mushroom. Sprinkle the mushrooms and spring onions lightly
with salt and cook in a lightly oiled stovetop grill pan, mushrooms stem side up, until
browned. Turn over and cook for 3 minutes.

To make the dressing, whisk together the lemon juice, soy sauce and mirin in a bowl.

Put the mushrooms, spring onions and lettuce in a large bowl and toss to combine. Drizzle
with the dressing, then gently fold to coat the salad in the dressing.

Preparation time: 10 minutes • Cooking time: 10 minutes • Serves 4 as a side salad

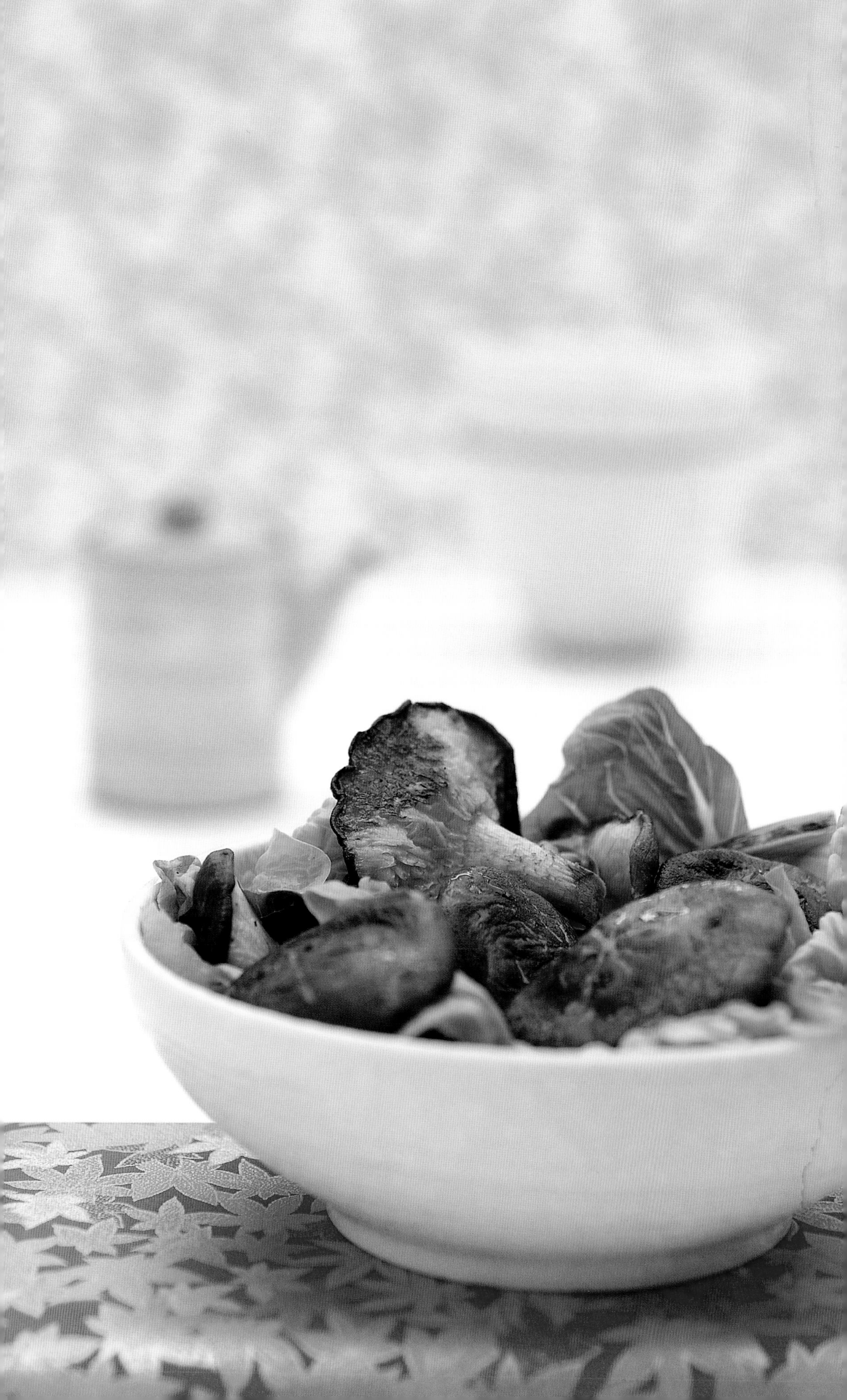

crab and cucumber sunomono

1 large cucumber, peeled, seeded and sliced
1 tablespoon (15 mL) sea salt
7 oz (200 g) fresh crabmeat
3 tablespoons (45 mL) rice vinegar
2 teaspoons (10 mL) lemon juice
2 teaspoons (10 mL) soy sauce
2 teaspoons (10 mL) superfine sugar
1 tablespoon (15 mL) dashi stock (see page 28)
1 teaspoon (5 mL) finely grated fresh ginger

Put the cucumber in a bowl, sprinkle with the sea salt and allow to stand for 30 minutes. Rinse and pat dry with absorbent kitchen paper.

Put the cucumber and crabmeat into a large bowl.

Whisk together the rice vinegar, lemon juice, soy sauce, sugar, dashi stock and ginger in another bowl until the sugar dissolves.

Pour the dressing over the salad and gently toss to coat.

Preparation time: 10 minutes, plus 30 minutes standing • Cooking time: None • Serves 4

spinach and wakame salad

½ oz (15 g) wakame
1 lb (500 g) baby spinach
3 tablespoons (45 mL) soy sauce
1 cup (250 mL) dashi stock (see page 28)
1 tablespoon (15 mL) bonito flakes
2 teaspoons (10 mL) toasted sesame seeds

Soak the wakame in a bowl of cold water for 10 minutes, then drain well and finely shred. Set aside.

Steam the spinach in a bamboo steamer set over a wok of simmering water for 5 minutes, or until it wilts, then plunge into iced water. Allow to cool slightly, then squeeze well to remove any excess moisture.

Combine the spinach and wakame in a bowl, then pile the spinach mixture into 4 mounds on serving plates.

Gently warm the soy sauce and dashi stock together in a saucepan and pour over the spinach. Sprinkle with the bonito flakes and sesame seeds and serve immediately.

Preparation time: 10 minutes, plus 10 minutes soaking • Cooking time: 10 minutes • Serves 4

sesame tuna tataki with sweet sake dressing

3 tablespoons (45 mL) sesame seeds
1 lb (500 g) piece fresh tuna
2 tablespoons (30 mL) sunflower oil
1¾ oz (50 g) mixed salad leaves
3 tablespoons (45 mL) pickled ginger, finely shredded

FOR THE DRESSING
½ teaspoon (2 mL) sesame oil
¼ teaspoon (1 mL) wasabi paste, or to taste
2 tablespoons (30 mL) rice vinegar
1 tablespoon (15 mL) superfine sugar
1 tablespoon (15 mL) mirin
1 tablespoon (15 mL) soy sauce

Put the sesame seeds on a large plate. Cut the tuna into 1¼ inch wide (3 cm) strips, brush lightly with a little of the sunflower oil and press to coat in the sesame seeds.

Heat the remaining sunflower oil in a frying pan, add the tuna and cook over a high heat for 1 minute on each side or until browned. Remove from the pan, wrap in plastic wrap and allow to cool for 15 minutes. Cut into thick slices.

Arrange the tuna in a fan shape on a serving plate and arrange the salad leaves in a mound in the center. Top with the pickled ginger.

To make the dressing, whisk together the sesame oil, wasabi paste, rice vinegar, sugar, mirin and soy sauce. Drizzle the dressing over the top.

Preparation time: 15 minutes • Cooking time: 5 minutes, plus 15 minutes cooling • Serves 4

Quickly sear the tuna on all sides,
then wrap in plastic wrap and rest for
2 minutes before slicing

SESAME TUNA TATAKI WITH SWEET SAKE DRESSING

soba, edamame, sweet potato and black sesame salad

10 oz (300 g) orange sweet potato, peeled and cut into wedges
1 tablespoon (15 mL) sunflower oil
15 oz (450 g) packet frozen soy beans or 7 oz (200 g) shelled
10 oz (300 g) dried soba noodles
2 spring onions, thinly sliced
2 tablespoons (30 mL) black sesame seeds

FOR THE DRESSING
1 tablespoon (15 mL) grated fresh ginger
2 cloves garlic, finely chopped
1 teaspoon (5 mL) sesame oil
1 tablespoon (15 mL) mirin
¼ cup (60 mL) rice vinegar
¼ cup (60 mL) soy sauce
1 teaspoon (5 mL) superfine sugar

Preheat the oven to 400°F (200°C). Put the sweet potato onto a baking tray, drizzle with the oil and bake for 20 minutes, or until soft.

Cook the soy beans in a large saucepan of boiling water until bright green and tender, then rinse under cold running water. Peel and discard the pods.

Cook the noodles in another large pan of boiling water until tender, then rinse under cold water. Transfer the noodles to a bowl of iced water and allow to stand while you prepare the rest of the salad.

To prepare the dressing, put the ginger, garlic, sesame oil, mirin, rice vinegar and soy sauce in a bowl and mix well to combine.

Put the drained noodles and sweet potato into a large bowl and add the soy beans, spring onions and black sesame seeds. Pour the dressing over and use your hands to toss the ingredients in the dressing until everything is coated.

Preparation time: 15 minutes, plus 10 minutes standing • Cooking time: 30 minutes • Serves 4

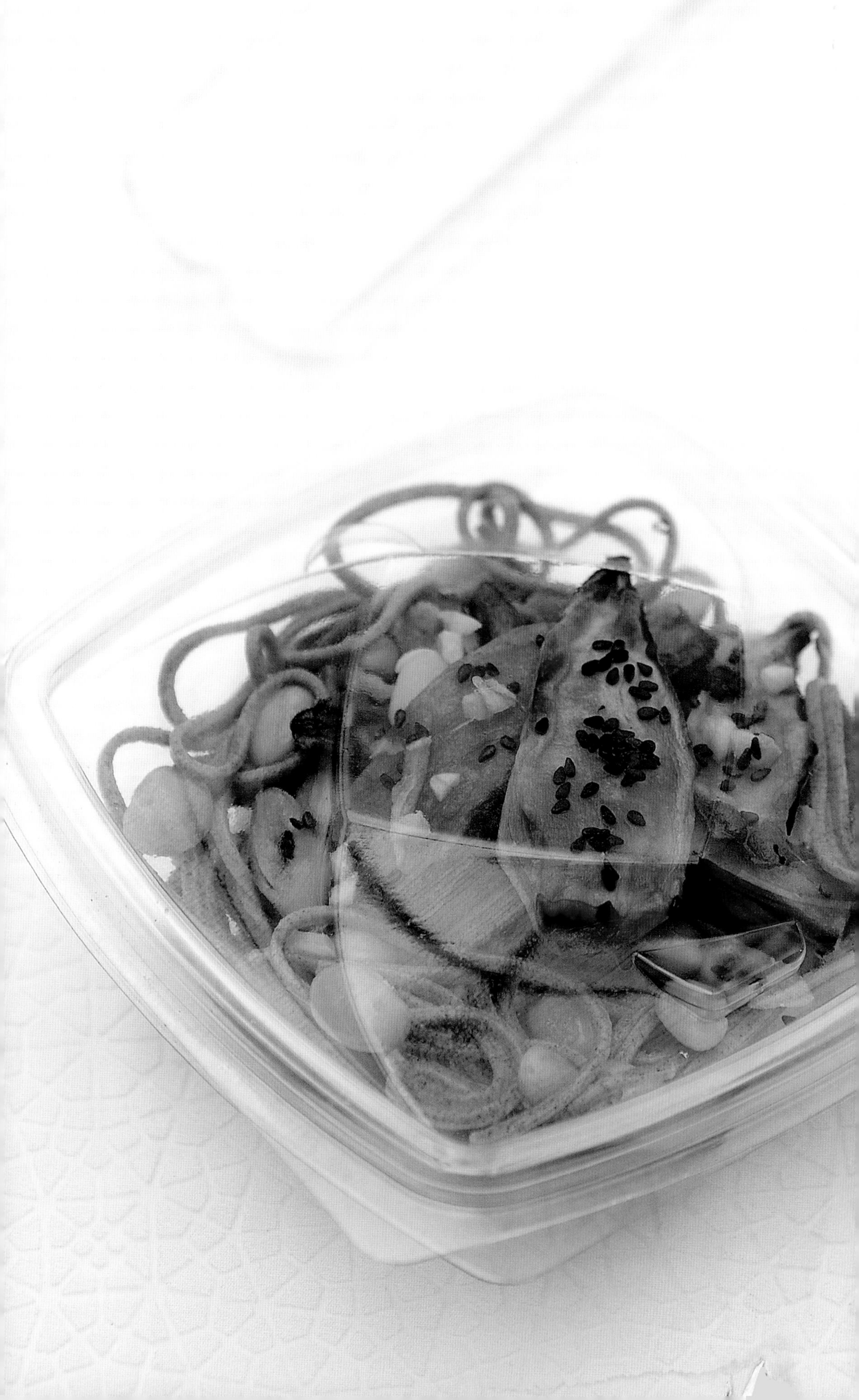

rare beef salad with miso dressing

1 lb (500 g) sirloin or rump steak
1 tablespoon (15 mL) vegetable oil
salt and freshly ground black pepper
1 carrot, peeled and finely shredded
1 daikon, peeled and finely shredded
shichimi togarashi powder, for sprinkling

FOR THE DRESSING
2 tablespoons (30 mL) red miso
1 tablespoons (15 mL) tahini
½ tablespoon (7 mL) mirin
1 tablespoon (15 mL) lemon juice
½ tablespoon (7 mL) superfine sugar

TO GARNISH
3½ oz (100 g) watercress
3 baby red radishes, thinly sliced

Rub the beef with a teaspoon of oil and season generously with salt and pepper.

Heat the remaining oil in a frying pan, add the beef and cook over a high heat for about
5 minutes, or until browned all over. Remove from the pan and wrap in foil, then allow to
stand for 10 minutes.

Put the carrot and daikon into a bowl and toss to combine.

To make the dressing, put the miso, tahini, mirin, lemon juice, sugar and 3 tablespoons
of water into a pan and cook over a low heat until combined. Remove and allow to cool
slightly. Thin with a little water until it reaches a pouring consistency.

Put the salad on individual serving plates, then slice the beef and arrange over the salad.
Drizzle with the dressing, garnish with the watercress and radishes and serve sprinkled with
shichimi togarashi powder.

Preparation time: 20 minutes, plus 10 minutes standing • Cooking time: 10 minutes • Serves 4

potato salad

3 large potatoes
1 large carrot, peeled
1 corn-on-the-cob
3 spring onions, sliced
1 cucumber, seeded and sliced into half moons
7 oz (200 g) smoked leg ham, sliced
1 cup (250 mL) Kewpie mayonnaise

Steam the potatoes, carrot and corn in a bamboo steamer set over a wok of simmering water for 10–15 minutes until tender. Allow to cool slightly, then peel the potato and break into large pieces.

Cut the carrot into thick slices and remove the corn kernels from the corn cob.

Add the carrot, corn, spring onions, cucumber, sliced ham and mayonnaise to the potato and gently mix until the vegetables are coated.

NOTE: In Japan potato salad is served using an ice-cream scoop.

Preparation time: 20 minutes • Cooking time: 10–15 minutes • Serves 4

simmered

Meat and vegetables simmered in a simple stock then dipped into a flavorsome dipping sauce, or fish and beef braised in a simple soy dashi stock, are not only easy to prepare, but they are low in fat and extremely nourishing.

osaka-style sukiyaki

6 eggs
2 tablespoons (30 mL) sunflower or vegetable oil
1 lb (500 g) marbled beef or pork, cut into very thin slices (ask your butcher to do this)
6 spring onions, sliced into short lengths
12 shiitake mushrooms
4 cabbage leaves, roughly chopped
10 oz (300 g) firm tofu, cut into bite-sized pieces
14 oz (400 g) fresh or dried udon noodles

FOR THE STOCK
½ cup (125 mL) sake
½ cup (125 mL) soy sauce

Lightly beat the eggs in a bowl and divide among 6 serving bowls.

Heat the oil in a large flameproof sukiyaki pan or electric wok, add the beef in batches and cook over a high heat for 3 minutes, or until browned.

Return all the beef to the pan, arrange the spring onions in one area of the pan and repeat with the remaining ingredients.

To make the stock, put 4 cups (1 liter) of water, the sake and soy sauce into a saucepan, bring to the boil and boil for 5 minutes to cook off the alcohol.

Add the stock to the sukiyaki pan or wok and bring to the boil, then reduce the heat to low and allow to simmer. Put on the table and serve. Each guest removes the meat and vegetables from the boiling stock and dips into a bowl of beaten egg before eating.

Preparation time: 20 minutes • Cooking time: 30 minutes • Serves 4–6

savory chicken prawn custard

7 oz (200 g) skinless chicken thigh fillets, diced
8 oz (250 g) green prawns, peeled, deveined and chopped
1 tablespoon (15 mL) watercress

FOR THE CUSTARD
3 eggs, lightly beaten
1½ cups (375 mL) dashi stock (see page 28)
1 teaspoon (5 mL) mirin
2 teaspoons (10 mL) soy sauce

Bring a large saucepan of water to the boil, then reduce the heat, add the chicken and prawns and simmer for 5 minutes. Remove from the heat, drain the chicken and prawns well and pat dry with absorbent kitchen paper.

To make the custard, combine the beaten eggs, dashi stock, mirin and soy sauce in a bowl, then strain through a fine sieve into another bowl and set aside.

Divide the chicken, prawns and watercress among 4 x ½ cup (125 mL) capacity ramekins with lids. Pour over the custard and cover with plastic wrap. Put the ramekins into a bamboo steamer set over a wok over simmering water, cover and cook over a low heat for 15 minutes. When the custard is set but still slightly wobbly in the center, cover and allow to stand for 2 minutes to set completely.

Preparation time: 15 minutes • Cooking time: 25 minutes • Serves 4

SAVORY CHICKEN PRAWN CUSTARD

If you don't have small ramekins with lids, use oven-proof dishes and cover them with plastic wrap or foil

kabocha squash simmered in a sake broth

1½ lb (750 g) kabocha squash
1 tablespoon (15 mL) sake
1 tablespoon (15 mL) mirin
1 tablespoon (15 mL) soy sauce
1 sheet inari, cut into thin strips
½ cup (125 mL) fresh cilantro sprigs

Roughly peel the squash leaving several patches of green skin. Remove the seeds and cut the flesh into large bite-sized pieces.

Put the squash into a large saucepan, add 2 cups (500 mL) of water, the sake, mirin and soy sauce and bring to the boil. Reduce the heat, cover and cook for 15 minutes, or until the squash is soft.

Serve the squash with the cooking liquid, sprinkled with the inari and cilantro.

Note: If you cannot find kabocha squash, butternut squash is a good substitute.

Preparation time: 20 minutes • Cooking time: 20 minutes • Serves 4

simmered

fish in soy and ginger

3 tablespoons (45 mL) finely shredded fresh ginger
¼ cup (60 mL) sake
¼ cup (60 mL) mirin
¼ cup (60 mL) soy sauce
1 lb (500 g) cod, halibut or monkfish fillets, cut into large pieces

Put the ginger, sake, mirin, soy sauce and ¼ cup (60 mL) of water into a deep frying pan, bring to the boil, then reduce the heat to a simmer.

Add the fish, cover with a lid and cook for 5 minutes, or until the fish is tender.

NOTE: This dish is usually served with freshly cooked rice and vegetables.

Preparation time: 15 minutes • Cooking time: 15 minutes • Serves 4

curry beef

1 tablespoon (15 mL) sunflower oil
1 onion, thinly sliced
1 tablespoon (15 mL) grated fresh ginger
2 cloves garlic, chopped
1 carrot, peeled and thinly sliced into half moons
1 packet Japanese curry (3½ oz/100 g), broken into pieces
1 lb (500 g) rump steak, thinly sliced

TO SERVE
steamed rice
pickled spring onions
red pickled ginger

Heat the sunflower oil in a large frying pan, add the onion, ginger and garlic and cook over a medium heat for 5 minutes, or until the onion is golden.

Add the carrot, 2½ cups (625 mL) of water and the broken curry block and cook, stirring, until the sauce comes to the boil and thickens.

Gradually add the steak, one piece at a time, to the curry sauce until it is all added, then cook for a further 5 minutes, or until the steak is tender.

Arrange the steamed rice over half a serving plate or bowl and add the curry to the other half. Repeat with the remaining plates or bowls. Serve with pickled spring onions and red pickled ginger.

Preparation time: 20 minutes • Cooking time: 15 minutes • Serves 4

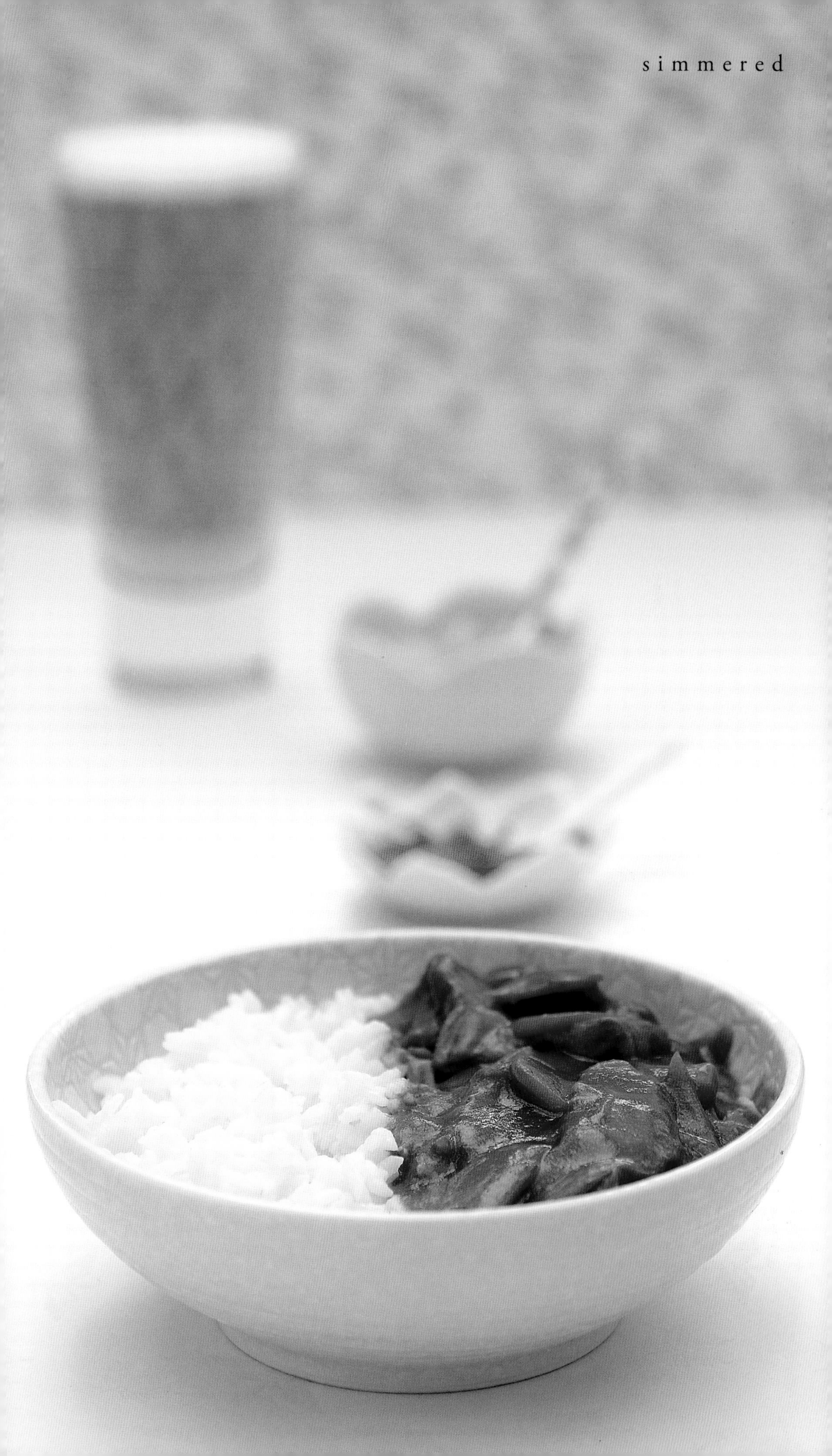

simmered

nabe

1–2 pieces kombu
2 lb (1 kg) skinless chicken thighs and drumsticks
10 oz (300 g) firm tofu, cubed
3 baby pak choi, halved
2 carrots, peeled and sliced
1 small daikon, peeled and cut into half moons

FOR THE SAKE PONZU DRESSING
3 tablespoons (45 mL) sake
1 tablespoon (15 mL) mirin
⅔ cup (160 mL) soy sauce
⅔ cup (160 mL) lemon juice

TO SERVE (OPTIONAL)
5 spring onions, finely sliced
shichimi togarashi powder

Put 6 cups (1.5 liters) of water into a shallow pot that can be kept warm on a table. Electric woks or fondue pots work well for this, or use a Chinese steam boat. Wipe the kombu clean using a damp piece of absorbent kitchen paper. Add to the water and allow to stand for 3 hours if time permits.

Cut the chicken into bite-sized pieces with a cleaver. Add to a large saucepan of simmering water and cook for 5 minutes. Remove the chicken with a slotted spoon, then rinse and pat dry with absorbent kitchen paper. Arrange the chicken on a large plate or allow each person to have their own plate. Neatly arrange the tofu, pak choi, carrots and daikon on another plate.

To make the dressing, put the sake and mirin into a small saucepan and boil for 2 minutes to cook off the alcohol. Remove from the heat and stir in the soy sauce and lemon juice. Divide the dressing among 4 dipping bowls.

Remove the kombu from the water with a slotted spoon and bring the water to the boil. Allow each person to cook their chicken and vegetables in the kombu-infused broth using slotted spoons, chopsticks or tongs and use the sake ponzu dressing as a dipping sauce. Serve the spring onions and shichimi togarashi powder, if using, on the side.

Preparation time: 20 minutes, plus 3 hours standing • Cooking time: 20 minutes • Serves 4

gyudon

2 cups (500 mL) dashi stock (see page 28)
2 tablespoons (30 mL) soy sauce
2 tablespoons (30 mL) mirin
1 tablespoon (15 mL) superfine sugar
2 tablespoons (30 mL) finely grated fresh ginger
1 onion, thinly sliced
14 oz (400 g) marbled beef, cut into very thin slices (ask your butcher to do this)
4 cups (1 liter) hot cooked rice
red pickled ginger, to serve

Put the dashi stock, soy sauce, mirin and sugar into a saucepan and bring to the boil, then reduce the heat to a simmer.

Add the onion and cook over a medium heat for 5–10 minutes, or until soft.

Add the beef and cook for a further 2–3 minutes, or until tender.

Divide the hot cooked rice among 4 serving bowls, then use a slotted spoon to remove the beef and onions from the stock and spoon over the rice. Ladle some of the stock over the beef, top with the ginger and serve.

Preparation time: 10 minutes • Cooking time: 12 minutes • Serves 4

simmered

shabu shabu

1–2 pieces kombu
1½ lb (750 g) marbled beef or pork loin, semi-frozen and sliced very thinly
8 leaves Chinese cabbage
10 oz (300 g) thinly sliced pumpkin, peeled
7 oz (200 g) bean sprouts
7 oz (200 g) shemiji mushrooms
3½ oz (100 g) enoki mushrooms

FOR THE SESAME SAUCE
⅓ cup + 1 tablespoon (100 mL) dashi stock (see page 28)
¼ cup (60 mL) sake
2 tablespoons (30 mL) mirin
2 tablespoons (30 mL) light soy sauce
1 teaspoon (5 mL) superfine sugar
6 tablespoons (90 mL) toasted white sesame seeds

TO SERVE
ponzu dressing (see page 134)
4 spring onions, finely sliced
shichimi togarashi powder
14 oz (400 g) hokkien noodles

Put 4 cups (1 liter) of water into a shallow pot that can be kept warm on a table. Electric woks or fondue pots work well for this or use a Chinese steam boat. Wipe the kombu clean using a damp piece of absorbent kitchen paper. Add to the water and allow to stand for 3 hours if time permits.

Cut the beef or pork into very thin slices and arrange on 4 individual serving plates or one large plate. Neatly arrange the vegetables on 4 serving plates or on a large platter.

Heat the dashi stock, sake, mirin, soy sauce and sugar in a saucepan, bring to the boil and cook over a high heat for 5 minutes, or until reduced slightly. Grind the sesame seeds in a suribachi or mortar and pestle until crushed, then add to the dashi mixture and mix well to form a sauce. Divide the sauce among 4 dipping bowls.

Remove the kombu with a slotted spoon and bring the water to the boil. Allow each person to cook their meat and vegetables in the broth and use the sesame sauce and ponzu dressing as dipping sauces. Serve the spring onions and pepper on the side.

When all the vegetables and meat have been cooked add the noodles to the boiling stock and cook for 5 minutes, then eat the noodles with the stock.

NOTE: Ask your butcher to prepare the meat for you or you can buy shabu shabu beef and pork from Japanese food stores.

Preparation time: 20 minutes, plus 3 hours standing • Cooking time: 20 minutes • Serves 4

If you don't have a suribachi you can
grind the sesame seeds in a spice grinder

simmered

SHABU SHABU

simmered

oyako don

1¼ cups (310 mL) dashi stock (see page 28) or chicken stock
½ cup (125 mL) light soy sauce
1½ tablespoons (22 mL) superfine sugar
10 oz (300 g) skinless chicken thigh fillets, chopped
3 spring onions, sliced
4 eggs
4 cups (1 liter) warm cooked rice

Put the dashi stock, soy sauce and sugar into a large saucepan and stir over a low heat until the sugar dissolves, then bring to the boil and reduce the heat to simmer.

Add the chicken and simmer for 5 minutes, or until tender, then add the spring onions and cook for a further 1 minute.

Lightly mix the eggs in a bowl, but do not beat. Pour the eggs into the pan around the chicken in one steady stream. Cook without stirring until the egg starts to bubble around the edge of the pan, then stir gently once.

Once the egg is almost set, divide the rice among 4 serving bowls and carefully spoon a piece of the chicken egg mixture onto the top of the rice.

Preparation time: 15 minutes • Cooking time: 20 minutes • Serves 4

desserts

Sweet finishes with authentically Japanese flavors, such as velvety green tea ice cream, the divine black sesame chocolate cake or the sumptuous creamy ginger cheesecake, are the perfect conclusion to any meal.

creamy ginger cheesecake with a green tea topping

4 oz (125 g) digestive cookies
2 tablespoons (30 mL) toasted sesame seeds
2 oz (60 g) butter, melted
3½ oz (100 g) crystallized ginger, chopped
1 lb (500 g) cream cheese, softened
⅔ cup (160 mL) superfine sugar
1 teaspoon (5 mL) vanilla extract
1 tablespoon (15 mL) lemon juice
4 eggs, lightly beaten

FOR THE TOPPING
2 teaspoons (10 mL) matcha powder
1 cup (250 mL) sour cream
½ teaspoon (2 mL) vanilla extract
2 tablespoons (30 mL) superfine sugar

Line the base of an 8 inch (20 cm) round springform tin with parchment paper. Put the cookies and sesame seeds into a food processor and process to form crumbs, then transfer to a bowl. Add the melted butter and stir to coat the crumbs in the butter. Spoon the mixture into the bottom of the tin. Allow to chill in the refrigerator for 20 minutes, or until firm. Sprinkle the ginger over the biscuit base.

Preheat the oven to 350°F (180°C). Beat together the cream cheese, superfine sugar, vanilla extract and lemon juice in a large bowl until smooth. Add the beaten eggs and beat to combine. Do not overbeat as this will cause the cheesecake to rise then fall on cooling.

Pour the mixture into the tin and bake for 45 minutes, or until just set.

To make the topping, whisk the matcha powder with 1 tablespoon (15 mL) of warm water in a small bowl until smooth. Put the green tea liquid, sour cream, vanilla extract and sugar into a large bowl and mix to combine. Spread over the top of the warm cheesecake, return to the oven and bake for a further 7 minutes. Allow to cool on a wire rack for 2 hours, then allow to chill in the refrigerator for 20 minutes, or until firm. Return to room temperature before serving.

Preparation time: 40 minutes, plus 20 minutes chilling • Cooking time: 55 minutes, plus 2 hours cooling • Serves 6–8

CREAMY GINGER CHEESECAKE WITH A GREEN TEA TOPPING

This dish is also delicious if stem (preserved) ginger is
used – chop it into small pieces so the crust won't fall
apart when you cut it to serve

green tea ice cream

1 cup (250 mL) milk
1½ tablespoons (22 mL) matcha
2 egg yolks
½ cup (125 mL) superfine sugar
1 cup (250 mL) heavy cream (35%)

Put the milk into a saucepan and heat until it is just about to come to the boil. Whisk together the matcha and a little of the warm milk in a bowl until smooth. Add to the remaining warm milk.

Lightly whisk the egg yolks and sugar in a heatproof bowl set over a saucepan of simmering water. Add the green tea milk and heavy cream and cook, stirring, over a medium heat for about 20 minutes until the custard coats the back of a wooden spoon.

Transfer the custard to a freezerproof container and freeze for about 1–2 hours, or until the edges start to freeze, then remove and beat with electric beaters. Repeat this process 3 times, or until the ice cream is smooth and creamy. Transfer the ice cream to the refrigerator 15 minutes before serving to let it soften slightly and make it easier to scoop.

Preparation time: 15 minutes, plus 6 hours freezing • Cooking time: 30 minutes • Serves 4

pancakes filled with red bean paste

2½ cups (625 mL) all-purpose flour
1 teaspoon (5 mL) baking powder
1 tablespoon (15 mL) superfine sugar
2¾ oz (80 g) butter, melted
3 eggs, lightly beaten
1½ cups (375 mL) milk
½ cup (125 mL) red bean paste
1¾ oz (50 g) butter
icing sugar, for sprinkling
vanilla ice cream, to serve (optional)

Sift the flour and baking powder into a large bowl and stir in the sugar. Make a well in the center.

Whisk together the butter, eggs and milk. Pour into the dry ingredients and whisk until just combined – the mixture should still be slightly lumpy.

Melt a little butter in a large non-stick frying pan, then spoon 1 tablespoon (15 mL) of the batter into the pan and allow to set slightly. Put 1 tablespoon (15 mL) of the red bean paste into the center of the pancake and spoon 1 tablespoon (15 mL) of the batter over the top to cover the filling. Turn and cook until golden brown and cooked through. Keep warm while you cook the remaining batter.

Sprinkle with icing sugar and serve warm with ice cream, if you like.

NOTE: These can also be cooked in a waffle maker.

Preparation time: 20 minutes • Cooking time: 20 minutes • Serves 4–6

black sesame chocolate cake

7 oz (200 g) butter, chopped, plus extra for greasing
1⅓ cups (330 mL) black sesame seeds
3 eggs, lightly beaten
1⅓ cups (330 mL) superfine sugar
¾ cup (125 mL) all-purpose flour
¼ teaspoon (1 mL) baking powder

FOR THE ICING
7 oz (200 g) dark chocolate, chopped
⅓ cup + 1 tablespoon (100 ml) light cream (10%)

Preheat the oven to 350°F (180°C). Grease and line an 8 inch (20 cm) square cake tin with parchment paper. Put the sesame seeds into a suribachi or spice mill and grind to form a smooth paste.

Put the butter and sesame paste into a saucepan and cook over a low heat until the butter melts.

Remove from the heat and stir in the eggs and sugar. Combine the flour and baking powder in a bowl. Sift the flour mixture over the egg mixture and gently fold to combine.

Pour the mixture into the prepared tin and bake for 35–40 minutes, or until a skewer comes out clean when inserted into the center. Allow to stand in the tin for 10 minutes before turning out onto a wire rack to cool completely.

Heat the chocolate and cream together in a saucepan over a low heat until the chocolate is melted. Remove from the heat and allow to cool for 15 minutes, or until the mixture thickens. Spread the chocolate icing over the cake and allow to set, then cut into small bars and serve.

Preparation time: 30 minutes • Cooking time: 50 minutes, plus 25 minutes cooling
• Serves 8–10

green tea macaroons filled with a light cream

7 oz (200 g) ground almonds
7 oz (200 g) icing sugar
2¼ oz (70 g) fresh egg whites, beaten
2 teaspoons (10 mL) matcha powder
⅔ cup (160 mL) heavy cream (35%)

FOR THE MERINGUE
6½ oz (190 g) granulated sugar
2½ oz (75 g) egg whites (older ones are better)

Preheat the oven to 300°F (150°C) and line 2 baking trays with parchment paper. Combine the ground almonds and icing sugar in a bowl, add the beaten egg whites and mix to form a sticky dough.

For the meringue, put the granulated sugar and ¼ cup (60 mL) water in a saucepan and boil to 250°F (121°C) (thread consistency) on a sugar thermometer. Whisk the egg whites in a clean bowl until soft peaks form. Continuing whisking the whites, gradually add the hot sugar syrup. Continue whisking at a moderate speed until the temperature of the meringue drops to between 113–104°F (45–40°C) on a sugar thermometer.

Put the almond dough into a large bowl and add the matcha powder. Add about a quarter of the warm meringue and mix to loosen the dough. Fold in the remaining meringue; it should drop from the spoon.

Spoon the mixture into a piping bag and pipe 2 inch (5 cm) circles onto the prepared baking tray, leaving some space between them to allow for spreading during cooking.

Lift the tray and tap the underside all over with your free hand. Each circle will spread a little and even out.

Bake for about 15–20 minutes, or until the base is crisp and lifts off the baking paper without sticking. Transfer to a wire rack and allow to cool.

Beat the cream until stiff peaks form. Sandwich 2 macaroons together using 1 teaspoon (5 mL) of the cream and serve.

NOTES: Unfilled macaroons will keep in an airtight container for 5 days. You can also fill the macaroons with lemon curd or mascarpone.

Preparation time: 40 minutes • Cooking time: 40 minutes • Serves 4

glossary

Ao nori
Tiny flakes of dried seaweed used as a condiment and sprinkled over salads, pancakes, stir-fries, okonomiyaki or soups.

Bonito flakes
This is dried fish that has been finely shaved and used to flavor soups and sauces. It is also used to give impact as a garnish.

Chinese cabbage
This cabbage has a delicate mustard flavor and is used in salads, soups and stir-fries.

Daikon
A long white radish, this can be pickled and used as a condiment, shredded and used as a garnish or sliced and cooked in stock.

Dashi
Buy dashi as granules and combine with water to make a quick and easy stock.

Dried shrimp
These are tiny dried shrimp, which vary in color and size and used in batters. Some are artificially coloured so check the ingredients.

Enoki
Small white mushrooms with long stems and a delicate flavor, they can be stir-fried or added to soups.

Hokkien
Thick yellow wheat noodles sold in the refrigerated section of Asian grocery stores. They are already cooked so just need reheating.

Japanese curry
This is sold in cardboard boxes in a chocolate-like bar. To use, break the block into pieces, add water and stir until thick.

Kewpie
The classic Japanese mayonnaise, it is used as a dipping sauce, squeezed over pancakes or as a filling in sushi.

Kombu
Long thick flat strips of dried seaweed used with bonito to make dashi stock.

Matcha
Also known as green tea powder, this is used in the traditional Japanese tea ceremony. It is also used in cakes and desserts. Blend with water or milk before using.

Mirin
A sweet rice wine with a lower alcohol content than sake (see below) and is used to give a glossy sheen to sauces and glazes.

Miso
This is a fermented soy bean paste, which comes in a variety of colors and flavors – usually the lighter the color the milder and sweeter the flavor.

Nori
Dried seaweed sheets, nori are best known as a major ingredient in sushi. Buy roasted sheets as they have a deeper flavor and store in an airtight container after opening.

Panko breadcrumbs
These are Japanese breadcrumbs, and are large shards of dried toasted bread used for crumbing meats and vegetables.

Pickled ginger
Thin slices of ginger pickled in salt and vinegar, they come in a variety of colors ranging from white to pink.

Potato starch
A white powdery flour used for coating meat and vegetables before deep-frying.

Ramen noodles
These are the classic noodles that cook in 2 minutes.

Red bean paste
This paste is made from cooked sweetened adzuki beans and is widely used in making Japanese sweets and desserts.

Rice vinegar
A clear rice wine vinegar, this is used in salad dressings.

S
, sake varies in quality
sk for cooking sake as
, and bring to the boil
e alcohol when using

T. .ted sesame oil used in dres g d sometimes for frying. Use sparingly as it as an intense flavour.

Ses
E .te sesame seeds are widely use Japanese dishes. Toast the white seeds before using.

Shichimi togarashi powder
There are many varieties of hot spice mixes you can sprinkle over meals. These are often served on condiment trays at restaurants to flavour your meal.

Shiitake mushrooms
Available fresh or dried these have an earthy mushroom flavour. Dried shiitake need soaking in hot water before cooking. Fresh are best suited to stir-frying.

Soba noodles
Dried buckwheat noodles, these are used in soups and as the main ingredient in zaru soba where the noodles are boiled, then chilled and served on a bamboo mat with a ponzu dipping sauce.

Soy sauce
Widely used in Japanese cooking, soy sauce varies in quality and saltiness. Try to use light soy sauce.

Sushi rice
Short pearly grains of rice used for making sushi. They are quite starchy, so rinse before use.

Tofu
Also known as bean curd, tofu comes in a variety of textures from silken, soft, medium to firm and silken firm.

Tonkatsu sauce
A sweet brown barbecue sauce served as a dipping sauce with tonkatsu or brushed on top of meats and pancakes before serving.

Udon noodles
These are white wheat noodles widely used in Japanese cooking mainly in soups.

Umeboshi plums
These are pickled Japanese apricots and are used as a filling in onigiri and sushi.

Wakame
Dried seaweed flakes, wakame has a salty spinach flavor.

Wasabi
Available in powder or paste, this is a peppery hot condiment widely used in Japanese cuisine. Use sparingly as it is powerful.

index

a c k n o w l e d g e m e n t s

Catie Ziller is again the first person to thank for this beautiful book. She has been in my life as my publisher for so many years, and her friendship, support and creative input are the reasons that keep me coming back to London year after year.

I would also like to thank the following: Emmanuel Le Vallois for his final design and the finishing touches he adds to each and every book, which make them stand out from the rest; my photographer, Clive Bozzard-Hill for the beautiful images and my designer, Jane Bozzard-Hill for laying out the book and allowing us into her home. I would like to thank the amazing Tracey Gordon for leaving her beloved home in Byron Bay, Australia and her divine son Kai for six weeks to come to the other side of the world to finish this book off with me; Tracey's brother, the awe-inspiring Peter Gordon for encouraging her to come and to make London an eating experience that I will cherish for the rest of my life, and Kathy Steer, my cherished editor, whom I still have not met after five years and who continues to ensure my recipes are written with amazing clarity and accuracy and make the end bit so easy – I always find it is such a pleasure working with you.

Thanks also goes to Sarah Tildesley who opened her home to me while I was in the UK – I am so happy to have you as a friend and a fellow food stylist/home economist/shopper/chief bottle washer; Lucas Purdy for sharing your home and your special girlfriend with me, and also a big thank you to my brother Matt, my sister-in-law Relle, Nathan and Rhearn for having my most cherished beloved dog, Pridey girl, for the duration of my stay in London.

My special thanks goes to my sister Annie who collects my mail, makes sure I pay my bills on time and sends me regular emails that help me feel connected to my home and all the things I love about where I live. Thank you to my incredible sister Paulie who travelled to Japan with me and helped me sample ridiculous quantities of food in a relatively limited period of time – you are such a fun, tolerant and durable travelling companion and I feel so fortunate to have you as my loving sister.

Lastly, thank you to all my friends who have provided me with a net for the last year that has helped keep me afloat – food is nothing without love – and you have given me so much of that, bless each of you.

UK Publisher: Catie Ziller
Author: Jody Vassallo
Photographer: Clive Bozzard-Hill
Illustrations: Alice Chadwick
Food for photography: Tracey Gordon
Art Editor: Jane Bozzard-Hill
Editor: Kathy Steer

ISBN 978-1-55285-971-1

Printed in China

09 10 11 12 13 5 4 3 2 1